Welcome to the EVERYTHING® series!

THESE HANDY, accessible books give you all you need to tackle a difficult project, gain a new hobby, comprehend a fascinating topic, prepare for an exam, or even brush up on something you learned back in school but have since forgotten.

You can read an EVERYTHING® book from cover to cover or just pick out the information you want from our four useful boxes: e-facts, e-ssentials, e-alerts, and e-questions. We literally give you everything you need to know on the subject, but throw in a lot of fun stuff along the way, too.

We now have well over 300 EVERYTHING® books in print, spanning such wide-ranging topics as weddings, pregnancy, wine, learning guitar, one-pot cooking, managing people, and so much more. When you're done reading them all, you can finally say you know EVERYTHING®!

Ⓔ Facts: Important sound bytes of information

Ⓔ Essentials: Quick and handy tips

Ⓔ Alerts!: Urgent warnings

Ⓔ Questions?: Solutions to common problems

THE
EVERYTHING®
— Series —

Dear Reader,

It was a challenge and a pleasure to write this book. As I wrote, selecting topics and a vocabulary that would be useful and interesting, I thought, "Who are you? A friend, a colleague, a student in a university class, such as I used to teach?"

Perhaps, I imagined, you are a recent graduate, starting out in life. On the other hand, now that your children are grown, you may be a mother rejoining the work force. You could also be a person seeking advancement in your present position. Nor would it surprise me if you are a senior citizen looking for mental stimulation. Age is not a barrier to acquiring new knowledge. Whoever you are, whatever your needs, this book is for you.

Learning is an adventure. As you travel through the pages of this book, bon voyage. May your journey be productive and enjoyable and may it lead to future adventures, success, and good fortune. Best wishes.

Sincerely,

Valentine Dmitriev Ph.D.

THE
EVERYTHING®
BUILD YOUR
VOCABULARY
BOOK

Over 400 words to help you
communicate with eloquence and style

Valentine Dmitriev, Ph.D.

Adams Media
Avon, Massachusetts

This book is dedicated with love and gratitude to my loving children
and their spouses: my daughter, Catherine, and her late
husband, Joe; my sons Michael and Alexander; and
my dear daughters-in-law, Carol and Susan.

• • •

An Everything® Series Book.
Everything® and everything.com® are registered trademarks of
F+W Publications, Inc.

Published by Adams Media, an F+W Publications Company
57 Littlefield Street, Avon, MA 02322 U.S.A.
www.adamsmedia.com

ISBN 10: 1-59337-531-X
ISBN 13: 978-1-59337-531-7
Printed in Canada
J I H G F E D C B A

Library of Congress Cataloging-in-Publication Data
Dmitriev, Valentine
The everything build your vocabulary book / Valentine Dmitriev.
p. cm. — (An everything series book)
ISBN 1-59337-531-X
1. Vocabulary—Problems, exercises, etc. 2. English language—
Grammar—Problems, exercises, etc. I. Title. II. Series: Everything series
PE1449.D59 2006
428.1—dc22

2006014736

This publication is designed to provide accurate and authoritative information with regard to the subject matter covered. It is sold with the understanding that the publisher is not engaged in rendering legal, accounting, or other
professional advice. If legal advice or other expert assistance is required, the
services of a competent professional person should be sought.

—From a *Declaration of Principles* jointly adopted by a Committee of the
American Bar Association and a Committee of Publishers and Associations

Many of the designations used by manufacturers and sellers to distinguish
their products are claimed as trademarks. Where those designations appear
in this book and Adams Media was aware of a trademark claim, the designations have been printed with initial capital letters.

This book is available at quantity discounts for bulk purchases.
For information, please call 1-800-872-5627.

THE

EVERYTHING

Series

EDITORIAL

Publishing Director: Gary M. Krebs

Director of Product Development: Paula Munier

Associate Managing Editor: Laura M. Daly

Associate Copy Chief: Brett Palana-Shanahan

Acquisitions Editor: Gina Chaimanis

Development Editor: Katie McDonough

Associate Production Editor: Casey Ebert

PRODUCTION

Director of Manufacturing: Susan Beale

Associate Director of Production: Michelle Roy Kelly

Cover Design: Paul Beatrice, Matt LeBlanc,
Erick DaCosta

Design and Layout: Colleen Cunningham,
Sorae Lee, Jennifer Oliveira

Visit the entire Everything® series at www.everything.com

Contents

Top Ten Ways to Improve Your Vocabulary / xii

Introduction / xiii

1

Chapter 1: Words for Work and Words for Home / 1

Getting Ready **2** • Workplace Words **2** • Shopping Vocabulary **8** • Banking and Business Words **10** • Talking with Friends **13** • Talking at Home **15** • Final Review **17**

2

Chapter 2: Mispronounced and Misused Words / 21

Initial Letter Mispronunciation **22** • Omitted Letters **27** • Wrongly Accented Syllables **31** • Accent on the Right Syllable **32** • Confusion Between Nouns and Verbs **35** • Misleading Homophones **39** • Final Review **40**

3

Chapter 3: Bad Grammar and Misused Phrases / 43

What Is Grammar? **44** • Tense Makes Sense **47** • The Future Tense: *Shall* and *Will* **48** • Consider the Case **53** • Pronouns, Verbs, and Case-Form Errors **54** • Pronouns: *Who, Whoever, Whom, Whomever* **55** • Preposition and Pronoun Errors **58** • Topic-Related Vocabulary **60** • Final Review **63**

4

Chapter 4: Broken Rules / 67

Simple but Troublesome Verbs **68** • The Trouble with Contractions **73** • The Dreaded Double Negative **76** • Misunderstanding *Lay, Lie,* and *Lie* **79** • Correct Speech **83** • Words of Wisdom **85** • Final Review **86**

5

Chapter 5: Personal Health and Medical Terminology / 91

You and Your Body **92** • When Health Problems Happen **95** • Choosing the Right Practitioner **98** • Other Health Care Professionals **100** • Understanding Diagnostic Tests **102** • Specialists and Dental Care **105** • Final Review **107**

6

Chapter 6: Pregnancy, Childhood, and Parenting / 111

Pregnancy and Birth **112** • A Child's Positive Characteristics **116** • A Child's Negative Characteristics **119** • Negative Parenting Styles **122** • Positive Parenting Styles **125** • Final Review **128**

7

Chapter 7: The Universe: Scientific Terminology / 131

Star Gazing **132** • Digging Deep **136** • Beneath the Sea **140** • The Invisible World **142** • Clouds and Weather **146** • Final Review **147**

8

Chapter 8: The Law and Legal Terms / 151

Marriage and Children **152** • Money Matters **155** • Wills and Estates **157** • Accidents and Lawsuits **160** • Victims and Crime **163** • A Day in Court **166** • Final Review **168**

9

Chapter 9: Power Words / 171

Business Meeting Words **172** • Job Application Words **173** • Business Troubles Vocabulary **176** • Pep Talk Words **178** • Daily Power Words **180** • Negotiation **182** • Final Review **185**

10

Chapter 10: Action and Event Words / 189

Positive Action Words **190** • Negative Action Words **192** • Naughty Action Words **194** • Happy Events **196** • Sad Events **199** • Disastrous Events **201** • Final Review **203**

11

Chapter 11: Appearance and Character Words / 207

Negative First Impressions **208** • Negative Physical Appearances **210** • Negative Personality Traits **211** • Positive First Impressions **214** • Positive Physical Appearance **216** • Positive Personality Traits **218** • Final Review **220**

12 **Chapter 12: Fine Arts Vocabulary / 223**

A Night at the Opera **224** • A Symphony Concert **225** • The Ballet **228** • A Visit to the Art Museum **231** • Color Vocabulary **234** • The Essence of Poetry **236** • Final Review **240**

13 **Chapter 13: Potpourri: Emotions and Essentials / 243**

Feelings and Emotions **244** • Phobias **248** • Essential Words **250** • Clichés **253** • Vulgarism, Profanity, and Slang **255** • Final Review **258**

14 **Chapter 14: International Languages / 261**

Latin and the Roman Empire **262** • French Words and Phrases **264** • Learning German **267** • Viva Italia **268** • Spain and Its Languages **271** • Russian Words **273** • Final Review **275** • Your Improved Vocabulary **276**

Appendix: Exercise Answer Key **277**

Acknowledgments

With much thanks, gratitude, and affection, I wish to acknowledge the following persons for their professional support and guidance. First on my list are the Adams Media editors. I thank Gina Chaimanis, who was always ready to answer my questions, to make helpful suggestions, and to resolve any problems that I encountered. Thank you, also, to editor Katie McDonough, whose expertise brought this project to a favorable conclusion. A special thank-you to my agent Mary Sue Seymour for her invaluable assistance in fostering my writing career. Many thanks to Irene Franett, Dottie Roberts, and the other members of the Lagoon Point Book Club for their interest and support. No acknowledgment would be complete without a word of gratitude to my son Alexander, Hilde Mott, Kelly Ess, Emily Miller, Kathy and Bob Rodgers, Jack Maxwell, and Judy Von Drachek for their computer skills and technical assistance. Another big thank-you to everyone who shared in the creative process of writing this book including my brother, Dmitry Stone, for his input as a marine biologist; Tom Heerhartz, for his knowledge of German; and my friend and colleague Patricia Oelwein.

Top Ten Ways to Improve Your Vocabulary

1.	Learn thirty new words in six days
2.	Learn new everyday workplace words
3.	Learn how to avoid misusing words
4.	Learn grammar etiquette the easy way
5.	Learn executive power words
6.	Learn medical terms pertaining to your body, your health, and your doctor
7.	Learn legal words you should know
8.	Learn what words to use when applying for a job
9.	Learn to speak correctly and confidently
10.	Learn foreign words and phrases everyone should know

Introduction

Communication is how we use words to interact with each other. We use words in order to inform, to gain information, to obtain what we need, to resolve problems, to express our feelings, and much more.

Your speech and the words you use define who you are. An effective use of words, the ability to say exactly what you mean, using and pronouncing essential words correctly gives you power and status.

In order to be a successful communicator and to get ahead in life, you may need to improve your vocabulary. The goal of this book is to provide you with the top essential words that every educated person should be able to use and define. A good vocabulary is, for example, likely to impress a potential employer if you're applying for a job. The use of appropriate words can help you communicate better with a doctor or dentist when you have a health problem.

Knowledge of legal terms is an essential tool when you need to read and understand a contract or confer with an attorney. Such knowledge can save you time and money and prevent costly mistakes.

Each chapter will contain word games, puzzles, exercises, and a list of words related to a specific category. For example, you will find chapters that offer essential medical, scientific, or legal terms.

There will be twenty or more essential words in each chapter. By the time you finish this book, you will have read, studied, and had the opportunity of learning more than 400 words. Some of the words may be familiar, but you have not been using them in your daily speech. In this case, a refresher course such as this book provides may be exactly what you need to prompt you to include these words when you write or speak, adding a spark and interest to your language. Whatever your vocabulary range may be, approach this book as a learning experience. We learn through action and participation. Reading the material as you would read a novel will not serve to improve your vocabulary.

To gain maximum benefit, give yourself at least six days to study each chapter. At this rate, you can learn up to five new words a day. To help you with your daily study, word lists, exercises, and puzzles will be divided into sections according to specific topics and headings with the expectation that a section can be completed within thirty to sixty minutes of study. All the words that you encounter will be defined with a guide to correct pronunciation. Sample sentences will demonstrate how your new vocabulary can be used in a conversation or in written material. Answers to specific exercises are given in the appendix. Approach this book and the knowledge it offers with a light heart. Do not fret if you are unable to complete an assignment in thirty or sixty minutes, or work through a chapter in six days. There is no time limit on how long it may take you to achieve your goal. Learning takes time. Remember that an improved vocabulary of 400 words begins with the acquisition of a single new word.

Chapter 1
Words for Work and Words for Home

Depending on their background, age, gender, place of employment, and lifestyle, people develop their own vocabulary. This vocabulary may fall into several categories. There are words that apply only to their jobs. For example, the terms used by a machinist, engineer, or construction worker are different from those used by a businessperson whose conversation may focus on projects, conferences, and reports. In a store, bank, or post office, the same individuals use another set of words. Among friends and at home, vocabularies become colloquial and casual.

Getting Ready

This chapter includes different words that are relevant to the workplace and other daily activities. Plan to study one section per day. Keep a notebook for writing words, working on exercises, and solving word games.

Like the athlete who takes time to warm up and flex his muscles before engaging in a strenuous activity, you will begin flexing your brain cells with a few basic word-play exercises. The purpose is to prepare you for the challenge of learning a new lexicon and to turn your thoughts to letters and sounds. Words are fun; they expand your mind. One letter, for example, can change the meaning of a word. The following exercises with letters and words will accelerate your mental responses as you journey through increasingly complex word play and new word acquisition games.

Workplace Words

There are many ways that you, depending on your job, can describe what you do and how you feel about your work. Since your goal is to improve and expand your vocabulary, this section will list words that are relevant to a workplace. Perhaps you'll find new words that express exactly what you may want to say about your boss, your coworkers, and your own job responsibilities. Before you begin studying the Workplace Words, Exercise 1 will give you a chance to see how many of the words you already know.

Exercise 1: Definitions: True or False?

Look at each vocabulary word in the left column and the definitions given for it. Determine if the definitions are true or false. Write *T* for true, *F* for false.

Word	Definition	T or F
arduous	Stubborn	_T_
diligence	Constant effort	_T_
echelon	Loud echo	___
inept	Awkward	___
egalitarian	Fair person	___

To check your answers, refer to the appendix or the following vocabulary list.

Word	arduous, adj.
Pronunciation	ar-du-ous
Definition	Exceedingly difficult or challenging

▶ *Drilling the tunnel is an arduous task.*

Word	diligence, n.
Pronunciation	dil-i-gence
Definition	Constant effort; hard work

▶ *The employee's diligence earned him a promotion.*

Word	echelon, n.
Pronunciation	ech-e-lon
Definition	Level of command

▶ *The company's upper echelon gave their approval.*

Word	egalitarian, adj.
Pronunciation	e-gal-i-tar-i-an
Definition	Believing in fairness and equality

▶ *An egalitarian boss treats all her employees fairly and doesn't show favoritism.*

Word	inept, adj.
Pronunciation	in-ept
Definition	Awkward, inefficient, unskilled

▶ *The nursing intern was too inept to remain in the program.*

Exercise 2: Write, Say, Define
Write the Workplace Words in your notebook. Study the pronunciation. Say the words. Write the definitions and indicate whether a word is a noun, a verb, or an adjective.

Exercise 3: Use the Words
Now it's time to use these words as much as possible when you speak to friends, colleagues, or family members. You can say, for example, "I learned five new words today. I will tell you what they are." Or, you could also use one of the words to talk about your work. Instead of saying, "I had a hard day," surprise your family by remarking in a more articulate manner, "I had an <u>arduous</u> day at the office."

More Workplace Words

Once you begin the study of a subject, it is important to review what you have learned the previous day before plunging ahead into new territory. Learning, as you may recall from your school days, involves understanding and memorization. As you become familiar with novel ideas, newly presented information, or a new vocabulary, your brain becomes much more receptive to retaining further knowledge if you take the time to review and practice what you have already learned. It's a good idea, therefore, to open your notebook and review the previously studied vocabulary before you turn to the next set of words.

 Essential

The word *inundate* comes from the Latin word inundatus. *Inundatus* originates from a combination of two words, *in*, which in Latin can mean either in or on, and the word *undare,* which means to overflow. Additionally, the word *inundate* that signifies overflow is derived from the Latin wave, *unda*. Thus from a combination of Latin words we get the English word *inundate.*

Your brain, like the rest of your body, is capable of achieving new skills. Physical exercise can strengthen your muscles and develop body control. With proper training, you can learn to swim, play tennis, play golf, play baseball, waltz, and even pirouette.

If you're not in the habit of using your mind to memorize poetry, song lyrics, obscure facts, or unfamiliar names, acquiring a new vocabulary can be a challenge. However, "practice makes perfect," and as you persevere, you'll soon discover that the task of committing words to memory will become increasingly easier to achieve and more satisfying.

Exercise 4: Definitions: True or False?

Look at each vocabulary word in the left column and the definition given for it. Determine if the definitions are true or false. Write *T* for true, *F* for false.

Word	Definition	T or F
inundate	To flood	____
meticulous	Made of metal	____
negligence	Drowsiness	____
tedium	Boredom	____
temerity	Shyness	____

To check your answers, refer to the appendix or the following vocabulary list.

Word	inundate, v.
Pronunciation	in-un-date
Definition	To flood; to overwhelm

▶ *Before long, the amount of daily mail would inundate the young secretary.*

Word	meticulous, adj.
Pronunciation	me-tic-u-lous
Definition	Giving exceedingly careful attention to detail

▶ *His job in the laboratory required meticulous performance.*

Word	negligence, n.
Pronunciation	neg-li-gence
Definition	Carelessness, neglect

▶ *His negligence cost him his job.*

Word	tedium, n.
Pronunciation	te-di-um
Definition	Tiredness, boredom

▶ *The tedium of her work was wearing her down.*

Word	temerity, n.
Pronunciation	te-mer-i-ty
Definition	Rash, bold behavior

▶ *He had the temerity to ask for a raise after failing to complete his assignment.*

Exercise 5: Write, Say, Define

Write the new words in your notebook. Study the pronunciation. Say the words. Write the definitions and indicate whether a word is a noun, a verb, or an adjective.

What You've Learned

You have now increased your vocabulary by ten. Remember to practice saying these words by including them in your conversations. As you drive to work or go about daily activities, repeat the words to yourself at every opportunity. Make up sentences and write down what you could say, using your new vocabulary.

Shopping Vocabulary

Your shopping vocabulary is limited to five words. Although you may not use them frequently, they are, nevertheless, essential words that every educated person should know and feel free to use when it is appropriate to do so.

Exercise 6: Definitions: True or False?

Look at each vocabulary word in the left column and the definition given for it. Determine if the definitions are true or false. Write *T* for true, *F* for false.

Word	Definition	T or F
apparel	Clothing	T
epicure	Beauty treatment	___
fetid	Greek cheese	___
haute couture	Fancy meal	___
memorabilia	Things worthy of remembrance	___

To check your answers, refer to the appendix or the following vocabulary list.

Word	apparel, n.
Pronunciation	ap-par-el
Definition	Clothing

▶ *She selected her business apparel with care.*

Word	epicure, n.
Pronunciation	ep-i-cure
Definition	A person with discriminating taste for food and wine

▶ *He was an epicure and favored only the finest French wines.*

Word	fetid, adj.
Pronunciation	fet-id
Definition	Unpleasant odor; smelly

▶ *The fetid contents of the Dumpster behind the grocery store revolted shoppers.*

Word	haute couture, n.
Pronunciation	haute cou-ture
Definition	French word meaning high fashion

▶ *She shopped only in boutiques that were haute couture.*

Word	memorabilia, n.
Pronunciation	mem-o-ra-bil-i-a
Definition	Things worthy of remembrance

▶ *Antique stores sell memorabilia.*

Exercise 7: Write, Say, Define

Write the Shopping Words in your notebook. Study the pronunciation. Say the words. Write the definitions and indicate whether the word is a noun, a verb, or an adjective.

What You've Learned

You have now extended your vocabulary by fifteen words. As you continue to improve your knowledge of essential words, do not neglect the words that you have already acquired. Remember to use as many of these words as you can as you go about your daily routines.

Banking and Business Words

These are the words that you may hear and want to use when you go to the bank and other business establishments. Refer to Exercise 8 and see how many of the words are familiar to you.

Exercise 8: Definitions: True or False?

Read the given definitions and determine if they are true or false. Write *T* for true, *F* for false.

Word	Definition	T or F
amortize	Embalm	_____
collateral	Property	_____
encumbrance	Embarrassment	_____
fiduciary	Embezzlement	_____
garnishment	Decoration	_____

To check your answers, refer to the appendix or the following vocabulary list.

Word	amortize, v.
Pronunciation	am-or-tize
Definition	To settle a debt by means of installment payments

▶ *It took him twenty years to amortize the mortgage on his house.*

Word	collateral, n.
Pronunciation	col-lat-er-al
Definition	Money or property pledged as security to ensure repayment of a loan

▶ *The bank loan was denied because the man didn't have the necessary collateral.*

Word	encumbrance, n.
Pronunciation	en-cum-brance
Definition	Anything that lessens the value of real estate or hinders the sale of property

▶ *The mortgage was an encumbrance that hindered the sale of his farm.*

Word	fiduciary, n.
Pronunciation	fi-du-ci-ar-y
Definition	A person or a bank that has a duty to act for the benefit of another person

▶ *When the child's parents died, the court appointed a fiduciary.*

Word	garnishment, n.
Pronunciation	gar-nish-ment
Definition	(a) A court order allowing a creditor to collect money or property in payment of a debt

▶ *When Jim failed to pay child support, he was served with a garnishment on behalf of his ex-wife.*

Word	garnishment, n.
Pronunciation	gar-nish-ment
Definition	(b) A decoration

▶ *Parsley is widely used as a food garnishment.*

Fact

The word *amortize* originates from the Old French word *amortize* which is the root of the term *amortir*, meaning to extinguish. You will notice that many English as well as French words have their origins in Latin. The word *amortize* is no exception, although in Latin it had a somewhat different meaning. In Latin the second syllable, *mortis*, means death.

Exercise 9: Write, Say, Define
Write the new words in your notebook. Study the pronunciation. Say the words. Write the definitions and indicate whether the word is a noun, a verb, or an adjective.

What You've Learned

You have now expanded your vocabulary by twenty words. Keep up the good work. Review your new words several times a day. Continue to use as many of the words in conversations as possible. Rattle off the words, entertaining friends and family. Remember if a word isn't used frequently, especially a new one, it is easily forgotten.

Talking with Friends

The words in this section, although relevant to the topic, will not be specific words that you might use as you talk with friends at a party. You already know how to converse with friends. The object of this section is to acquaint you with words that describe a person's manner of speaking, and the prevalent mood and behavior at a merry gathering with friends.

Exercise 10: Definitions: True or False?

Read the given definitions and determine if they are true or false. Write *T* for true, *F* for false.

Word	Definition	T or F
colloquial	Somber	_____
conviviality	Friendly gathering	_____
frivolity	Lighthearted behavior	_____
jocular	Vein in the neck	_____
libation	A drink	_____

To check your answers, refer to the appendix or the following vocabulary list.

Word	colloquial, adj.
Pronunciation	col-lo-qui-al
Definition	Characteristic of written or spoken communication (words) that is breezy or informal

▶ *Conversation among friends is generally colloquial.*

Word	conviviality, n.
Pronunciation	con-viv-i-al-ity
Definition	The enjoyment of a friendly gathering to feast and drink and socialize

▶ *The festive conviviality of the dinner party appealed to him.*

Word	frivolity, n.
Pronunciation	fri-vol-i-ty
Definition	Lighthearted, silly behavior

▶ *The dean disapproved of the students' frivolity after the game.*

Word	jocular, adj.
Pronunciation	joc-u-lar
Definition	Joking, witty, amusing

▶ *His jocular account of his adventure was very entertaining.*

Word	libation, n.
Pronunciation	li-ba-tion
Definition	The act of pouring out wine, or other liquid; humorously, a drink

▶ *The host offered wine as a libation to his friends.*

Exercise 11: Find the Right Word
Complete the blanks by finding the right word from the previous table.

1. _ _ b _ _ i _ n

2. _ o _ u _ a _

3. c _ _ v _ _ _ a _ _ _ y

4. _ _ l _ _ q _ _ _ l

5. _ r _ _ o _ _ t _

Exercise 12: Write, Say, Define
Write the new words in your notebook. Study the pronunciation. Say the words. Write the definitions and indicate whether a word is a noun, a verb, or an adjective.

What You've Learned

You have now completed the next-to-the-last section of Chapter 1. With five more words to study in the following pages, you will have attained your first goal: the acquisition of twenty–thirty words per chapter. I hope you have been successful in remembering and continuing to practice the new vocabulary that you have acquired.

Talking at Home

The emphasis here will be not on the words that are commonly used in speaking to family members. Such words will not be unfamiliar to you and will not help you in expanding your vocabulary. For this reason, the focus will be on terms that describe behaviors and interactions that are likely to exist within a family.

Exercise 13: Definitions: True or False?

Read the given definitions and determine if they are true or false. Write *T* for true, *F* for false.

Word	Definition	T or F
appellation	Title	_____
approbation	Disapproval	_____
decorum	Riot	_____
disparagement	Verbal abuse	_____
filial	Children's relationship to their parents	_____

To check your answers, refer to the appendix or the following vocabulary list.

Word	appellation, n.
Pronunciation	ap-pel-la-tion
Definition	A name or title

▶ *The appellation her brother used to tease Nancy made her angry.*

Word	approbation, n.
Pronunciation	ap-pro-ba-tion
Definition	Praise; approval

▶ *Family members value each other's approbation.*

Word	decorum, n.
Pronunciation	de-co-rum
Definition	Good social behavior; dignified conduct

▶ *In public their children behaved with decorum.*

Word	disparagement, n.
Pronunciation	dis-par-age-ment
Definition	Verbal abuse

▶ *Parental disparagement can seriously damage a child's self-esteem.*

Word	filial, adj.
Pronunciation	fil-i-al
Definition	Relating to a child's relationship with his or her parents

▶ *It was his filial duty to honor his parents.*

Exercise 14: Write, Say, Define

Write the Talking at Home Words in your notebook. Study the pronunciation. Say the words. Write the definitions and indicate whether a word is a noun, a verb, or an adjective.

Final Review

As you near the end of this chapter and your first set of new vocabulary words, you can review what you're learning by completing the following word-play exercises: Antonyms, Synonyms, and Hidden Words.

 **Essential**

> Antonyms are words that have opposite or nearly opposite
> meaning. For example, the antonym for *hard* is *soft*. *Hot* is
> the antonym for *cold*. Can you think of other antonyms?

Exercise 15: Antonyms

In the following list, read the words in the left column and
then write an antonym for each word to the right. Answers
may vary.

Word	Antonym
arduous	_____
inept	_____
diligence	_____
egalitarian	_____
tedium	_____
meticulous	_____
negligence	_____
temerity	_____

To check your answers, refer to the appendix.

Exercise 16: Synonyms

Read the words in the left column and write a synonym for each word to the right.

Word	Synonym
apparel	_____
fetid	_____
haute couture	_____
memorabilia	_____
amortize	_____
collateral	_____
garnishment	_____
encumbrance	_____

To check your answers, refer to the appendix.

 Fact

Synonyms are one of two or more words that have the same or nearly the same meaning. For example, a *candy* could also be called a *sweet*. The words *work*, *toil*, and *labor* are synonyms. Can you think of some other examples?

Exercise 17: Find the Hidden Words

Example: Inundate: in, inn, it, nun, nude, neat, unit, unite, dine, due, duet, dean, den, din, date, ate, and, an, at, tin, tune, tide, tad, tan, ten, tea, eat, end.

Alert!

Most words have smaller, hidden words within them. Look for hidden words in your new vocabulary. Hint: start with the first letter of a word and see how many hidden words start with that letter. Continue the exercise using, in sequence, all the letters in the main "parent" word.

Copy the following word list into your notebook. Leave plenty of space between the words where you can write the hidden words you find. You should be able to find as few as 5 to as many as 150 hidden words.

1. colloquial
2. conviviality
3. frivolity
4. jocular
5. libation
6. appellation
7. approbation
8. decorum
9. disparagement
10. filial

Chapter 2
Mispronounced and Misused Words

The English language has many pitfalls for the speaker who wishes to avoid misusing words. Many words sound similar but are spelled differently and have different meanings. Problems occur when a noun is confused with a similar-sounding verb or when two words are spelled identically yet whose meanings become clear only when used in a sentence. There is also the problem of mispronouncing words. In some cases, the errors occur as the result of careless speech patterns and poor enunciation, while in others, it is due to lack of knowledge.

Initial Letter Mispronunciation

Linguists who study the English language have identified approximately one hundred commonly mispronounced or misused words. One common mispronunciation occurs through the inadequate enunciation of the initial letters of the word, especially words beginning with v, t, or the combination of t and h as in *th*. This chapter will focus on the mispronunciation of these initial letters. The top thirty mispronounced and misused words will be considered.

Mispronunciation of the Initial V

Words beginning with v are frequently mispronounced. In these cases, the v is mistakenly spoken as a w. The following table gives an example of how this error affects one's speech.

Correct	Incorrect
vacuum	Pronounced as *wacuum*
visual	Pronounced as *wisual*
vacation	Pronounced as *wacation*

Exercise 1: Definitions: True or False?

Read each word in the left column and the given definition for it. Determine if the definition is true or false. Write *T* for true, *F* for false.

Word	Definition	T or F
vacuous	Huge	_____
vehement	Strong emotion	_____

Word	Definition	T or F
vestige	Garment	_____
vicarious	Lively	_____
voracious	Greedily hungry	_____

To check your answers, refer to the appendix or the following table.

Word	vacuous, adj.
Pronunciation	vac-u-ous
Definition	Lacking substance; that which is empty

▶ *His speech was a vacuous repetition of old slogans.*

Word	vehement, adj.
Pronunciation	ve-he-ment
Definition	Strongly felt; highly emotional; forceful

▶ *She was vehement in her battle to rescue homeless animals.*

Word	vestige, n.
Pronunciation	ves-tige
Definition	Something that is no longer common; something that is lost

▶ *The last vestige of the wrecked boat was swept away by the tide.*

Word	vicarious, adj.
Pronunciation	vi-car-i-ous
Definition	Feelings that arise from experience of others rather than one's own experience

▶ *Violent movies gave the boys a vicarious thrill.*

Word	voracious, adj.
Pronunciation	vo-ra-cious
Definition	Greedily hungry for food or other things that give pleasure

▶ *Jane, a voracious reader, borrowed stacks of books from the library every week.*

Exercise 2: Write, Say, Define

Write the *v* words in your notebook. Study the pronunciation. Say the words. Write the definitions and indicate if the word is a noun, a verb, or an adjective.

 Essential

> If you have access to a tape recorder use it to evaluate how you pronounce the initial letters *v, t* and *th*. Speaking in your natural voice read and record the following words: *Vision, vacant, viper, vicar, voice, this, that, them, these, those, they, time,* and *temper.* Replay your tape and listen to how you speak. Determine if you need to enunciate the initial letters more carefully.

Mispronouncing *T* and *Th*

This error in pronunciation is also a very common mistake made by people who fail to enunciate the initial *t* or *th* of a word correctly. When these mispronunciations occur, the *t* and *th* are slurred, making them sound like *d*. This is an extremely careless way of speaking and reflects negatively on the speaker. The following table gives an example of how these errors affect one's speech.

Correct	Incorrect
that	Pronounced as *dat*
together	Pronounced as *dah-gether*
them	Pronounced as *dem*

Exercise 3: Definitions: True or False?
Read each of the *t* and *th* words in the left column. Determine if the given definitions are true or false. Write *T* for true, *F* for false.

Word	Definition	T or F
tantamount	Equal to	_____
technocracy	Form of government	_____
theocentric	Circular	_____
thespian	Actor	_____
tome	Small tent	_____

To check your answers, refer to the appendix or the following vocabulary list.

Word	tantamount, adj.
Pronunciation	tan-ta-mount
Definition	Equal to, as in value or significance

▶ *When he gave her the engagement ring, it was tantamount to a marriage proposal.*

Word	technocracy, n.
Pronunciation	tech-noc-ra-cy
Definition	Government by engineers, technicians, or other highly skilled members of society

▶ *The theory of technocracy was greatly popularized in the 1930s.*

Word	theocentric, adj.
Pronunciation	the-o-cen-tric
Definition	Placing God in the center of a belief

▶ *The theocentric sermon of the preacher inspired his congregation.*

Word	thespian, n.
Pronunciation	thes-pi-an
Definition	An actor

▶ *He was a fine Shakespearian thespian.*

Word	tome, n.
Pronunciation	tome
Definition	A thick, heavy book, usually a scholarly work

▶ *The professor spent many years writing his tome on evolution.*

Exercise 4: Write, Say, Define

Refer to the previous table. Write the words and definitions in your notebook. Study the pronunciation. Say each word five times, enunciating the initial letters clearly. Indicate whether a word is a noun, a verb, or an adjective.

What You've Learned

You have now concluded the sections that focused on the mispronunciation of the initial letter in a word, especially words that begin with the letters *v*, *t*, and *th*. Although this may appear to be a minor mistake, anyone with a good knowledge of the English language would quickly recognize these errors in your speech and that might be to your disadvantage. Improving a vocabulary by learning more words would seem to be of little value to individuals who allow small, careless mispronunciations to mar their speech.

It is hoped that as you progress through this book, you will continue to review and practice the vocabulary that you have already acquired, paying close attention to how these words should be used and spoken.

Omitted Letters

Another mispronunciation occurs when a speaker omits, or swallows, letters within a word. This happens when someone fails to pronounce all the letters that make up a particular word. It appears to listeners as if a letter or letters remained unspoken in the speaker's throat, hence the term *swallowed*. This is a common occurrence. If you listen carefully to TV announcers or even political candidates, you're bound to hear several words with swallowed letters. For anyone who wishes to speak as an intelligent, educated person, such sloppy use of the English language is not acceptable.

The following table gives an example of how a word can be corrupted by the omission of a letter.

Correct	Incorrect	Omitted Letter
spiel	spill	e
number	numer	b

Exercise 5: Find the Omitted Letters

Study the following table of correctly and incorrectly spoken words. Indicate in the blank space which letter has been swallowed. Answers are in the appendix.

Correct	Incorrect	Omitted Letters
arctic	actic	_____
recognize	reconize	_____
government	goverment	_____
February	Febuary	_____
commensurate	commesurate	_____

Tricky Words

You will now have another set of vocabulary words to study and to add to your growing knowledge of the English language. These are also tricky words, because some of their letters can be easily swallowed by a careless speaker. To avoid such errors, study them and learn to articulate them properly. The following table will show you how letters in the tricky words can be unconsciously omitted.

 Fact

It's very likely that you already own a dictionary and perhaps, as you acquired a new vocabulary, you have referred to it from time to time. If, however, you would like to purchase another dictionary, the *American Heritage Dictionary* would be a good choice.

Exercise 6: Find the Omitted Letters
Study the following table. Note the correct and incorrect pronunciation. Indicate the omitted letters. Answers are in the appendix.

Correct	Incorrect	Swallowed Letters
iniquity	inquity	_____
innocuous	innocous	_____
obsequious	obsequous	_____
penultimate	penutimate	_____
rudimentary	rudmentary	_____

Exercise 7: Write, Say, Define

Write the following tricky words in your notebook. Study the pronunciation. Say the words. Write the definitions and indicate if the word is a noun, a verb, or an adjective.

Word	iniquity, n.
Pronunciation	in-iq-ui-ty
Definition	Injustice; immoral behavior

▶ *It was an iniquity to sentence the innocent man.*

Word	innocuous, adj.
Pronunication	in-noc-u-ous
Definition	Harmless; bland; lacking drama

▶ *Labeled as a drama, the play was so innocuous it closed after the first performance.*

Word	obsequious, adj.
Pronunication	ob-se-qui-ous
Definition	Servile; submissive in order to please superiors

▶ *The obsequious employee failed to attain the favors he sought.*

Word	penultimate, adj.
Pronunication	pen-ul-ti-mate
Definition	Next to the last

▶ *The separation was penultimate to the breakup of the marriage.*

Word	rudimentary, adj.
Pronunciation	ru-di-men-ta-ry

Definition   Basic; the first slight beginning of
something

▶ *The piano lesson began with rudimentary finger exercises.*

What You've Learned

By now you should be aware of the mispronunciation
that occurs when initial letters or letters within a word are
either pronounced incorrectly or simply omitted (swallowed). In order to avoid making these mistakes, monitor
your own speech and listen critically to other speakers.
Noting errors that you may hear in their delivery will help
you abstain from making similar mispronunciations yourself.

 Essential

Chapter 3 will take you a step farther than this chapter,
as you consider the frequent and regrettable misuse of
phrases and sentences. While addressing this problem,
you will have the opportunity of adding thirty more
new words to your growing vocabulary.

Wrongly Accented Syllables

As languages evolve, specific ways of pronouncing words
become the norm. The way we speak, the words we use,
and especially how these words are pronounced become
a standard by which our peers, our superiors, and our

subordinates measure our intelligence, our level of education, and our social status. It's a fact of life that if the elite majority of a country and the dictionaries agree on how a word should be pronounced, that becomes the proper, "educated" way of speaking.

One of the greatest problems that foreigners as well as students of new words encounter is not knowing which syllable to accent in a given word. If such an uncertainty exists in your mind, your best resource is the dictionary. However, in many cases, people blithely mispronounce words, seemingly unaware how others say the same words, and rarely, if ever referring to a dictionary.

The following table gives examples of how common, familiar words are frequently mispronounced by persons who accent the wrong syllables.

Wrong	Right	Accented Syllable
po-litical	po-li-tical	li
ad-ver-tise-ment	ad-ver-tise-ment	ver
vi-ta-min	vi-ta-min	vi
a-dage	ad-age	ad
im-po-tent	im-potent	im
im-portant	im-por-tant	por

Accent on the Right Syllable
In this section the focus will be on accenting the right syllable, as well as learning new words.

Exercise 8: Which Syllable?

Read the following list of words and underline what you believe to be the right syllable to accent.

1. abdicate   4. despotism

2. aberration   5. serendipity

3. cartel

To check your answers, refer to the appendix or the following vocabulary list.

Word	abdicate, v.
Pronunciation	ab-di-cate
Definition	To give up; to step down from a high position

▶ *There are times when a ruler must abdicate to save his life.*

Word	aberration, n.
Pronunciation	ab-er-ra-tion
Definition	A deviation from the right course or standard

▶ *Tom's tantrum was an aberration from his usual compliant behavior.*

Word	cartel, n.
Pronunciation	car-tel
Definition	An organization seeking to control a market, or a political group united for a particular cause

▶ *The oil cartel controls our gasoline prices.*

Word	despotism, n.
Pronunciation	des-pot-ism
definition	A dictatorship

▶ *The people suffered under the monarch's despotism.*

Word	serendipity, n.
Prounciation	ser-en-dip-i-ty
Definition	A fortunate coincidence

▶ *Finding an expensive new dress at the consignment shop was pure serendipity.*

Exercise 9: Write, Say, Define

Write the new words in your notebook. Note the accented syllables and pronunciations. Correct mistakes. Say the words, enunciating properly. Indicate whether a word is a noun, a verb, or an adjective.

What You've Learned

At this point, with the completion of the preceding section on wrongly accented syllables, you have added twenty new words to your vocabulary. This gives you a total of fifty words. It is important to review your entire vocabulary every day. Pay special attention to words that you may have difficulty remembering. Some words like some facts are easier to remember than others. Concentrate on the *meanings* of words. Once you fully understand what a word means and how it can be used in a sentence, it is much more likely to become an established familiar word in your spoken and written vocabulary.

Confusion Between Nouns and Verbs

It must be remembered that nouns are words that denote a person, place, thing, condition, action, or quality. Verbs, unlike nouns, are not static. They denote action and can be varied to describe present, past, and future actions. Confusion and errors occur because some nouns and verbs are very similar in spelling and pronunciation. Such similar-sounding words are called homophones.

Sometimes a noun can, with modifications, be used as a verb. For example, the word *shout* is used as a noun in the following sentence: A <u>shout</u> echoed through the night. By adding *ed* to the noun *shout,* it becomes a verb as illustrated in the next sentence: The crowd <u>shouted</u> when Tom made a touchdown. By the same token, certain verbs can be used as nouns.

This section will acquaint you with a few of the most commonly misused pairs of similar-sounding nouns and verbs. These are words that can be used only as nouns or verbs. You will see that the words in the following table are pairs of nouns and verbs that are similar in spelling and sound. Your task will be to differentiate between the nouns and verbs and use them correctly in a sentence. Sometimes both noun and verb are identical and are distinguished only by how they are pronounced or used.

Noun	Verb
advice	advise
effect	affect
essay	assay
convoy	convey
object	object (oppose)

Exercise 10: Select the Right Noun or Verb

Study the words in the preceding table. Depending on the context of the following sentences, circle the proper word to complete the sentence.

1. I need (advice, advise), can you help me?
2. He gave me good (advice, advise)
3. I hope my attorney will (advice, advise) me.
4. I will try to (advice, advise) you.
5. The (effect, affect) of the fire was terrifying.
6. She wondered how the fire would (effect, affect) her parents.
7. Your kind words (effect, affect) me deeply.
8. The (effect, affect) of his speech was negligible.
9. The boy worked on his (essay, assay) all afternoon.
10. The miner went to (essay, assay) his gold nugget.
11. The man hurried to (essay, assay) his ore findings.
12. Johnny wrote a fine (essay, assay).
13. The (convoy, convey) left at dawn.
14. Please (convoy, convey) my regards to your father.
15. I tried to (convoy, convey) the urgency to my sister.
16. How can I (convoy, convey) this to him?

Exercise 11: Select the Word Object

Use the word *object* as a noun or a verb. Use it correctly and underline the syllable that is accented, depending on whether the word is used as a noun or a verb.

1. The _____ came in a brown bag.

2. I _____ to this proposal.

To check your answers, refer to the appendix or the following vocabulary list.

Word	advice, n.
Pronunciation	ad-vice
Definition	Counsel; a given opinion

▶ *He gave me good advice.*

Word	advise, v.
Pronunciation	ad-vise
Definition	To offer advice or counsel

▶ *I advise you to stop following me.*

Word	affect, v.
Pronunciation	af-fect
Definition	To cause an emotional response

▶ *His drinking started to affect our relationship.*

Word	effect, n.
Pronunciation	ef-fect
Definition	A result, something brought about by a cause

▶ *The effect of the beautiful music was to bring tears to her eyes.*

Word	assay, v.
Pronunciation	as-say
Definition	To evaluate

▶ *It was important to assay his ore deposits.*

Word	essay, n.
Pronunciation	es-say
Definition	A written composition

▶ *He wrote an essay on the magnificence of the Rocky Mountains.*

Word	convey, v.
Pronunciation	con-vey
Definition	To carry; to transport or communicate

▶ *He was told to convey a message to the general.*

Word	convoy, n.
Pronunciation	con-voy
Definition	An escort, especially for the protection of armed forces

▶ *The convoy escorting the troopship left at dawn.*

Word	object, n.
Pronunciation	ob-ject
Definition	A thing

▶ *The object was a pretty toy.*

Word	object, v.
Pronunciation	ob-ject
Definition	To oppose

▶ *I object to this proposal.*

What You've Learned

The misuse of homophonic nouns and verbs is a common mistake because the spelling and the sound of the words are almost identical. For this reason, it is important to pay attention to the one or two letters that may be different within a similar pair. For example, the noun *effect* is written with *e* at the beginning. The verb *affect* begins with *a*. By keeping these slight differences in mind, you can avoid making mistakes when you are using same-sounding nouns and verbs.

Misleading Homophones

Homophones are words that sound the same but have different meanings and uses. In the preceding section, you were introduced to homophonic nouns and verbs (e.g., one word of the pair was a noun, the other a verb).

Misleading homophones can be more confusing because there is no distinction between nouns or verbs. In other words, there can be similar-sounding pairs of nouns as well as verbs. Adding to this possible confusion is the fact that many of the homophonic words can be used as nouns or verbs. For example the noun *compliment,* which means "to praise with a pleasant remark," can also be used as a verb. He <u>complimented</u> the cook's fine dinner. *Complement,* *compliment*'s homophone, refers to that which completes or perfects something. It is a noun that can also be used as a verb. The graphs were a <u>complement</u> (noun) to her report. The graphs <u>complemented</u> (verb) the report.

Final Review

Now you have the opportunity of testing yourself to see how much you have learned as you come to the end of this chapter. The following Word Play Exercises will test your skill and help you review and retain the new words that you have added to your vocabulary.

Exercise 12: Find the Words

Read the given definitions and fill in the blanks, completing the words that match the definitions.

1. Market-controlling organization: c __ __ t __ __

2. Deviation from usual behavior: __ b __ r __ __ t __ __ n

3. Resign a high position: __ b d __ __ a __ e

4. Happy coincidence: s __ __ __ n __ __ p __ __ y

5. Dictatorship: __ __ s p __ __ __ s m

Exercise 13: Fill in the Blank

Write in the missing first letters.

1. __ome

2. __estige

3. __oracious

4. __icarious

5. _ _ espian

6. _ehement

7. _antamount

8. _acuous

9. _ _eocentric

10. _echnocracy

Exercise 14: Write the Homophone

Read the words in the left column, and then write their homophones in the blank space.

1. advice _____

2. effect _____

3. essay _____

4. convey _____

5. complement _____

Exercise 15: Complete the Words

Read the partial words in the left column and add the missing letters to complete the word.

1. iniq _ _ _ _

2. innocu _ _ _

3. obseq _ _ _ _ _ _

4. penult _ _ _ _ _

5. rudi _ _ _ _ _ _ _

To check your answers, refer to the appendix.

Chapter 3
Bad Grammar and Misused Phrases

The misuse of phrases is a common mistake even among well-spoken, educated people. The problem stems from not paying enough attention to what they are saying or from disregarding the rules of grammar. Nevertheless, persons who want to improve their vocabulary and advance in their career or profession must make the effort to recognize and correct these lapses in their speech. This chapter gives examples of the most commonly misused phrases. Exercises and word games offer a better understanding of the basic rules of grammar.

What Is Grammar?

Grammar has been called a science of language. However it's not a science in the same sense as biology or chemistry, which are entities that can be subjected to research and development. Grammar can also be called a discipline because it focuses on words, the relationships between words, and how words are used to express a thought in a sentence.

More accurately, perhaps, a grammar book could be called a book of language etiquette. One well-known writer on socially correct behavior was Emily Post. Her book on etiquette minutely described all the aspects of proper behavior, from what to wear, to what to say, to which fork to use at a formal dinner. Armed with her book of instructions, a person would be ready to have tea at the White House or visit the Queen of England with complete confidence and propriety.

Grammar's function is similar as far as the use of a language is concerned. It teaches proper written and verbal behavior. Every language has its own set of grammatical rules. Many languages are far more complex than English from the standpoint of how words are used in sentences. Nevertheless there are rules, and it is grammar's task to teach us how to combine words in a sentence so that the thought is expressed in a socially and educationally appropriate manner. Basically, grammar etiquette explains how to avoid misusing verbs and other parts of speech. Our goal is to learn how to use "good grammar" versus "bad grammar" when we write or speak.

Parts of Speech

The following table explains the main parts of speech in the English language.

Part of Speech	Function
noun	To name anything that exists
pronoun	To stand in place of, or represent, a noun
adjective	An added word, descriptive of a noun
verb	An action word that controls all expression of thought; no sentence is complete without a verb
adverb	A word that intensifies or lessens the meaning of a verb
preposition	A word that shows the relationship of a verb to a noun or pronoun; such as *between, of, or, for*
conjunction	A word that joins words in a sentence; such as *and, or, but*

Grammar Vocabulary

The following table contains some useful Grammar words, their pronunciations, and their definitions.

Word	connotation, n.
Pronunciation	con-no-ta-tion
Definition	An idea that gives the meaning of a word and also what it implies (e.g., a positive or negative emotional response to the word)

▶ *The connotation of the word* refuse *is less negative than that of the word* reject.

Word	denotation, n.
Pronunciation	de-no-ta-tion
Definition	The meaning of a word as found in a dictionary

▶ *The* denotation *of the word* elation *is happiness.*

Word	etymology, n.
Pronunciation	et-y-mol-o-gy
Deifinition	The history of words; the study of word origins

▶ *The etymology of the English language is a fascinating subject.*

Word	semantics, n.
Pronunciation	se-man-tics
Definition	The meaning of something, especially words

▶ *The semantics of a student's vocabulary test were incorrect.*

Words	syntax, n.
Pronunciation	syn-tax
Definition	The part of grammar that deals with the arrangement and relationship of words in a sentence

▶ *According to syntax, the subject of a sentence comes before the verb.*

Exercise 1: Write, Say, Define

Write the Grammar Vocabulary in your notebook. Note the pronunciation. Say the words and write their definitions.

Essential

> Grammar's first task is to define the function of the various categories of words in our vocabulary. Its second task is to show how these different words interact with each other and the role that they play in a sentence. Grammatically speaking, words that make up a language are called parts of speech.

Tense Makes Sense

In grammar, the word *tense* is an indication of time as expressed by a verb in a sentence. In English there are three tenses: the present, the past, and the future. To indicate a specific tense, the verbs change in accordance with the intended meaning of a sentence. For example, the verb *to go* in the present tense changes to *went* in the past tense. In order to indicate a future event, the words *shall*, *will*, and *to be* are added to a verb that remains in the present tense. For example, he will go home tomorrow. To reiterate, if a verb does not indicate a tense properly, especially in the past tense when a verb may be radically changed, the speaker or writer is using "bad grammar."

The following table lists some common past-tense errors:

Incorrect	Correct
He come yesterday.	He came yesterday.
She say goodbye.	She said goodbye.

Incorrect	**Correct**
She look good last week.	She looked good last week.
He phone last night.	He phoned last night.

The verbs *to come* and *to say* change to <u>came</u> and <u>said</u> in the past tense; they are known as irregular verbs. The other two verbs, *look* and *phone,* are known as regular verbs. The past tense of regular verbs is always indicated by the addition of *ed* at the end of the verb.

Exercise 2: Write the Present Tense

Study the past tense of the following verbs. Write the present tense of the verbs in the provided blank space.

1. ate   _____
2. went   _____
3. spoke   _____
4. was   _____
5. were   _____
6. slept   _____
7. had   _____
8. read   _____
9. verified   _____
10. fought   _____

To check your answers, refer to the appendix.

The Future Tense: Shall *and* Will

The future tense of a verb is always indicated by placing the words *shall, will,* or *to be* before the verb. To express a future intention or expectation, it is correct to use *shall* in the first person and *will* in the second and third persons.

In grammar, the terms *first, second,* or *third person* are used to show a change in a pronoun or verb to indicate whether a person is speaking, is spoken to, or is being spoken about. I come (first person). You come (second person). He <u>comes</u> (third person). Note the change in the verb (*to come*) in the third-person form. To speak correctly, remember that a verb, indicating a third person, that is singular in the present tense always undergoes a change.

 Fact

> In present-day speech, with the common use of the contraction *'ll* for either *shall* or *will,* this distinction between the two words becomes blurred and almost irrelevant. Nevertheless, as an educated person, one should be aware of the proper use of *shall* and *will* as words denoting the future tense of verbs.

To express future determination, a command, or a promise, the words *shall* and *will* are reversed. *Will* is used in the first person; *shall* is used in the second and third person.

The following table presents the use of *shall* and *will* in Simple Futurity (Future):

Singular	Plural
I shall go	We shall go

Singular	Plural
You will go	You will go
He will go	They will go

The next table presents *shall* and *will* as suggesting determined intention:

Singular	Plural
I will marry him.	We will succeed.
You shall do as I say.	You shall stay here.
He shall obey me.	They shall go.

Exercise 3: Convert Present Tense to Past Tense

Study the following list of verbs. Write their past tense in the provided blank space.

1. play   _____
2. lay   _____
3. run   _____
4. grow   _____
5. leave   _____
6. try   _____
7. fly   _____
8. know   _____
9. glow   _____
10. expect   _____

To check your answers, refer to the appendix.

Try It Out

Some verbs, you may have noticed, vary greatly in their past tense from how they are written in the present tense. This variability can account for frequent misuse of words when a person is speaking about something that happened in the past. Such errors may be even more significant than the confusion between *shall* and *will* as indicators of future actions or events.

Here is a table of Past, Present, and Future Vocabulary, their pronunciations, and their definitions:

Word	advent, n.
Pronunciation	ad-vent
Definition	A first or new appearance

▶ *The advent of spring lifted her spirits.*

Word	antiquity, n.
Pronunciation	an-tiq-ui-ty
Definition	Ancient times

▶ *The museum of antiquity contains relics of life in the Middle Ages.*

Word	contemporary, adj.
Pronunciation	con-tem-po-rar-y
Definition	Existing at the present time

▶ *She enjoyed reading contemporary literature.*

Word	eventuality, n.
Pronunciation	e-ven-tu-al-i-ty
Definition	Something that may happen

▶ *In the eventuality of a merger, I may lose my job.*

Word	forebode, v.
Pronunciation	fore-bode
Definition	Predict; foretell

▶ *The dark clouds forebode a storm.*

Word	imminent, adj.
Pronunciation	im-mi-nent
Definition	Something ready to happen, usually evil or bad

▶ *After the attack, war was imminent.*

Word	modernism, n.
Pronunciation	mod-ern-ism
Definition	A practice or usage particular to modern times

▶ *Modernism as a movement to adopt religion to modern thought appealed to him.*

Word	obsolete, adj.
Pronunciation	ob-so-lete
Definition	Outmoded; no longer in use

▶ *Slang words used in the twenties are now obsolete.*

Word	posterior, adj.
Pronunciation	pos-te-ri-or
Definition	Later in time

▶ *The accident was posterior to his drinking too much beer.*

Word	retrospection, n.
Pronunciation	ret-ro-spec-tion

Definition   The act of recalling the past

▶ *Talking about his youth, the old man indulged in retrospection.*

Exercise 4: Write, Say, Define

Read the previous vocabulary words. Write the words in your notebook. Study the pronunciation. Say the words and write their definitions. Indicate if a word is a noun, a verb, or an adjective.

Consider the Case

In grammar, the word *case* shows how a noun or pronoun relates to a verb. Nouns have only two forms to show case: the common or uninflected case, and the possessive case. The words *common* and *uninflected* mean that the noun used in a sentence remains unchanged. When a noun is used in a possessive case, it is inflected; in other words, it is changed. An apostrophe and an *s* are placed at the end of the word. For example, the following nouns show the possessive case: the boy's car, Mary's doll, Mother's hat.

All pronouns, except the third-person neuter pronoun *it,* have three forms to show case. They are the common, the possessive, and the objective cases. Pronouns are often misused in sentences, especially when the intention of the speaker is to show an objective case. Refer to the following table of pronouns and case forms for clarification.

Common Case	Possessive Case	Objective Case
First-person singular I	my/mine	me
Second-person singular you	your	you
Third-person singular he, she	his, her	him, her
First-person plural we	our	us
Second-person plural you	your	you
Third-person plural they	their	them

 Essential

> The neuter pronoun *it* has only two forms to show case: uninflected *it* and the possessive form *its*. Note that the *it* in the possessive case has no apostrophe before the *s*. The word *it's* is a contraction for *it is*. The misuse of *its* (possessive) with *it's*, a contraction, is a common written mistake.

Pronouns, Verbs, and Case-Form Errors

The use of pronouns can be tricky. Errors occur when a pronoun and a verb are mismatched. This happens when a pronoun from the objective case is used as the subject of a verb. Note the following sentence, "John and him went fishing." The pronoun *him* is in the objective case; it does not belong as part of the subject of the sentence. The subject of the sentence is always in the common case. Moreover, the subject of a sentence always precedes the verb. The common case of a third-person-singular pronoun is either he or she. Correctly, the same sentence should read: John and he went fishing, not John and him.

Alert!

Please note that the singular and plural second-person pronoun *you* remains unchanged in both the common and the objective case. The only change appears in the possessive form. At this time, the pronoun *you*, both singular and plural becomes *your*. Example: Your class, or all of you, must bring your notebooks.

Another common mistake arises when a speaker uses a common-case pronoun—such as *he, she*, or *I*—when the sentence calls for the objective-case form of a pronoun—*him, her*, or *me*. The first thing to remember is that any pronoun that appears after a verb is always in the objective case. To illustrate: Nancy gave the book to him, or her, or me not, as some people say, Nancy gave the book to I, or to he and she.

Pronouns: **Who, Whoever, Whom, Whomever**

Who and *whoever, whom* and *whomever* are pairs of pronouns that are frequently misused. *Who* and *whoever* are common-case pronouns. They are used as subjects in a sentence. *Whom* and *whomever* are objective. They are the objects of a verb. "Who called? Who is that man? The man who works with me is retiring." In all these instances, the word *who* is in the common case. The same applies to the pronoun *whoever*. The following sentences show the proper way of using the objective *whom*. "I met my niece whom I like very much. Whom will you hire?" Whom is in the objective case because the question is asking: "You will hire whom?" "I shall hire whomever I choose" is another example of the objective case.

Exercise 5: Select the Proper Pronouns and Verb

Read the following sentences. Cross out the misused verbs and pronouns. Write the correct words in the provided space.

1. She and him are good friends. _____

2. I (will, shall) vote for the person I want. _____

3. The man whom phoned me is my uncle. _____

4. Blessed are them who pray. _____

5. Whom shall I say is calling? _____

6. The horse hurt (its, it's) leg. _____

7. Him and they caught a fish. _____

8. Who will you marry? _____

9. He and her are coming soon. _____

10. Give this to whomever comes first. _____

To check your answers, refer to the appendix.

Try It Out

You have now completed the section on grammar errors that occur when the wrong pronoun is used in the context of a sentence. The common, the possessive, and the objective cases were discussed. It was emphasized that the pronoun in a sentence must match the intended case of what is said or written. In other words, there must be agreement between verbs and pronouns. See the following table of Possession Vocabulary:

Word	acquisition, n.
Pronunciation	ac-qui-si-tion
Definition	The act of obtaining or gaining possession of something

▶ *His art collection was a valuable acquisition.*

Word	appropriate, v.
Pronunciation	ap-pro-pri-ate
Definition	To take possession of

▶ *The bank will appropriate my car if I don't make my payments on time.*

Word	appurtenance, n.
Pronunciation	ap-pur-te-nance
Definition	Something belonging to another thing of greater importance

▶ *The gazebo was an appurtenance to her property.*

Word	ownership, n.
Pronunciation	own-er-ship
Definition	Legal possession

▶ *No one questioned her ownership of the estate.*

Word	proprietor, n.
Pronunciation	pro-pri-e-tor
Definition	The owner or manager of a business establishment

▶ *The pub's proprietor was a cheerful man.*

Exercise 6: Write, Say, Define

Read the Possession word list. Write the words in your notebook. Study the pronunciation. Say the words and write the definitions. Indicate if a word is a noun, a verb, or an adjective.

Preposition and Pronoun Errors

A preposition is a word that is used to show the relationship of one noun or pronoun to another in a sentence: "The dog stood between Mary and me." The preposition *between* shows how the noun *Mary* relates to the pronoun *me*. One thing to remember is that a pronoun following a preposition is always in the objective case. Persons who forget this rule make the mistake of using a pronoun in the common case instead of one in the objective case. At other times people make the grammatical error of using objective-case pronouns as subjects of a sentence rather than common-case pronouns.

For example, <u>him</u> and <u>her</u> are in love. This sentence is wrong. The pronouns *him* and *her* are in the objective case but are used as subjects of the sentence; that usage calls for common-case pronouns. The sentence should read: <u>He</u> and <u>she</u> are in love.

An equally glaring mistake is made when the first pronoun is used correctly in the objective case while the second pronoun is not. If you listen to people talking, you are bound to recognize these errors, now that you know how these mistakes occur and what they are.

For example, the man thanked <u>him</u> (correct) and <u>I</u> (incorrect). The sentence should read: The man thanked <u>him</u> and <u>me</u>. Both pronouns correctly show the objective case. Remember common-case pronouns come *before* a verb. Objective-case pronouns come *after* a verb.

Exercise 7: Pronouns in the Objective Case

Complete the following sentence by writing pronouns that show the objective case. Choose a different pronoun for each sentence. Example: He looked at <u>me</u>.

1. I sat by _____.

2. Come. Sit beside _____.

3. This is for _____ and _____.

4. The present was from _____.

5. He will go with _____.

To check your answers, refer to the appendix.

What You've Learned

This concludes the section on common preposition and pronoun errors. As you learned, mistakes indicate a disagreement between the context of a sentence, the preposition, and a pronoun, if the pronoun denotes a wrong case. It is hoped that you'll be able to recognize these errors, whether they are written or spoken, and avoid them in your own speech.

Topic-Related Vocabulary

In the preceding section, you were reminded that in the objective case, the noun or pronoun is subordinate to the verb and a preposition, when used. In life we may find ourselves in a subordinate position at work, out socially, and at home. There may also be individuals who are subordinate to us. The following vocabulary list offers words that imply subordination.

Word	hoi polloi, n.
Pronunciation	hoi pol-loi
Definition	From the Greek meaning masses, general population

▶ *The aristocracy felt superior to the hoi polloi.*

Word	maladroit, adj.
Pronunciation	mal-a-droit
Definition	Awkward; inept; unskilled; of low status

▶ *The maladroit maid worked hard to learn new skills and to raise her station in life.*

Word	servitude, n.
Pronunciation	ser-vi-tude
Definition	A condition of bondage; compulsory labor forced upon prisoners

▶ *The felon's servitude lasted a year.*

Word	subjugate, v.
Pronunciation	sub-ju-gate
Definition	To dominate; to bend to one's will

▶ *The dictator aimed to subjugate his people.*

Word	subservient, adj.
Pronunciation	sub-ser-vi-ent
Definition	Submissive; humble

▶ *The master expected his slaves to be subservient.*

Exercise 8: Write, Say, Define

Read the Subordinate vocabulary. Write the words in your notebook. Study the pronunciation. Say the words. Write the definitions and indicate whether a word is a noun, a verb, or an adjective.

As you know, the purpose of this book is to improve your vocabulary. In doing so, its aim is also to call your attention to grammatical errors, mispronunciation, and general misuse of words. Most of the new words that you studied in this chapter were related to this topic. The following list of Language-Related Vocabulary is similar in this respect.

Word	lexicon, n.
Pronunciation	lex-i-con
Definition	Vocabulary of a language; a dictionary

▶ *The law student used a Latin lexicon.*

Word	linguist, n.
Pronunciation	lin-guist
Definition	One skilled in languages

▶ *My uncle is a linguist. He speaks seven languages.*

Word	morphology, n.
Pronunciation	mor-phol-o-gy
Definition	A part of grammar that deals with word formation

▶ *The study of morphology taught her the structure and origin of words.*

Word	philology, n.
Pronunciation	phi-lol-o-gy
Definition	The scientific study of languages

▶ *He was a professor of philology at Cambridge.*

Word	vernacular, n.
Pronunciation	ver-nac-u-lar
Definition	A spoken form of language; common everyday speech

▶ *It took time for her to learn the vernacular French spoken in a village outside of Paris.*

Exercise 9: Write, Say, Define

Read the Language-Related Vocabulary list. Write the words in your notebook. Study the pronunciation. Say the words, write their definitions, and indicate if a word is a noun, a verb, or an adjective.

Final Review

Now you will be given the opportunity to review your new vocabulary and to test your skill at completing the following memory and brainteaser-review problem exercises.

Exercise 10: Definition Review

Read the given definitions and give the correct word by filling in the blanks. To check your answers, refer to the appendix.

1. The definition of a word in a dictionary: d __ n __ __ __ __ __ __ __

2. The implied meaning of a word: c __ __ n __ __ __ __ t __ __ __

3. The study of word origins: __ __ y __ __ l __ __ __

4. No longer in use: __ b __ o __ __ t __

5. Recalling the past: __ __ t r __ __ p __ c __ __ __ n

6. Refers to the present: c __ __ t __ m __ o __ __ __ __

7. The theory of keeping up with the times: m __ __ e r __ __ __ m

8. The meaning of things, especially words: s __ __ a __ __
__ c __

9. Ancient times: __ n __ __ __ u __ __ y

10. Grammatical relationship and arrangement of words: __ y
__ __ __ x

Exercise 11: Complete the Words.
Fill in the blanks by adding the right letters to complete
the words. To check your answers, refer to the appendix.

1. adv __ __ __

2. event __ __ __ __ __ __

3. fore __ __ __ __

4. imm __ __ __ __ __

5. post __ __ __ __ __

6. subj __ __ __ __ __

7. mala __ __ __ __ __

8. __ __ __ v __ __ __ __ __

9. hoi __ __ __ __ __ __

10. __ u b __ e __ v __ __ n __

Exercise 12: Find the Hidden Words

Read the list of words in the left column. Write them in your notebook and find at least ten hidden words within each word. Then play a game with yourself and see how many more hidden words you can find.

1. acquisition
2. appropriate
3. appurtenance
4. proprietor
5. ownership

Exercise 13: Fill in the Blank

Complete the words by filling in the first two missing letters. To check your answers, refer to the appendix.

1. _ _ nguist

2. _ _ ilology

3. _ _ xicon

4. _ _ rphology

5. _ _ rnacular

The focus of this chapter was on how words are misused when grammar rules are broken. Grammar governs how words should relate to each other. Once a person understands the function of the different parts of speech, it becomes much easier to avoid grammatical errors. The chapter addressed the importance of using the right verb to indicate tenses (i.e., the present, the past, or the future). The proper use of pronouns and how they relate to verbs as well as prepositions in both the common and objective cases was also discussed. If you already have a good understanding of grammar and can clearly identify the difference between good and bad grammar, then you are aware that there are additional grammatical misuses of words and phrases that need to be addressed. The mismatch of verbs, nouns, and pronouns in positive as well as in negative sentences will be covered in Chapter 4.

Chapter 4
Broken Rules

The man before the judge was pleading his case. He was articulate and appeared to be intelligent until he misspoke. "They was building a fence," he said. That one small mistake diminished him in the eyes of the court and weakened his defense. Verbs are tricky, and they can trip you if you've forgotten grammar rules that govern their correct use. In this chapter you will learn new vocabulary words as well as how to avoid verbal errors.

Simple but Troublesome Verbs

There are five simple, basic verbs that are among those most commonly misused by individuals who are either careless in their speech or who haven't learned the fundamental rules of good grammar. The verbs in question are *to be, to do, to have, to go,* and *to get.* Once again, remember that the tenses and verbs must be in agreement with all the parts of speech in a sentence. The man in the courtroom made the mistake of using the singular past tense of the verb *to be* (*was*) with the plural pronoun *they.* He should have used the plural past tense form of *to be,* which is *were.* Had he done so, the verb and pronoun would have been in agreement and he would have spoken correctly.

See the following table of verbs and pronouns:

Verb	Pronouns			
To be	I	you	he, she, it	we, you
Present tense	*am*	*are*	*is*	*are*
Past tense	*was*	*were*	*was*	*were*
To do	I	you	he, she, it	we, you
Present tense	*do*	*do*	*does*	*do*
Past tense	*did*	*did*	*did*	*did*
To have	I	you	he, she, it	we, you
Present tense	*have*	*have*	*has*	*have*
Past tense	*had*	*had*	*had*	*had*

To go	I	you	he, she, it	we, you
Present tense	*go*	*go*	*goes*	*go*
Past tense	*went*	*went*	*went*	*went*

To get	I	you	he, she, it	we, you
Present tense	*get*	*get*	*gets*	*get*
Past tense	*got*	*got*	*got*	*got*

 Fact

> The word *conjugation*, as you may recall from an English class, refers to the orderly arrangement of a verb, indicating the changes that may occur depending upon the tense in a sentence and the verb's relation to a noun or pronoun.

As you studied the preceding table, you should have noticed that the major inflections (changes in words) occur in the verb *to be* as it relates to the singular pronouns: *I, you, he, she,* and *it.* The inflection *are* applies to all the plural pronouns, including the pronoun *you,* whether that pronoun is singular or plural. In the past tense the word *was* is used with all singular pronouns and *were* is used with all plural pronouns.

The remaining four verbs—*to do, to have, to go,* and *to get*—are uninflected in the present tense (all the words remain unchanged), except for the third-person singular:

he, she, or *it*. In the case of the third-person singular, an *s* is added to the verb *to get* and an *es* to the verbs *to do* and *to go*. Again, in the third-person singular, the verb *to have* changes to *has*. You should also remember that in the past tense these four verbs keep the same past-tense word (e.g., *did, had, went,* and *got*), regardless of which singular or plural pronoun is used.

Exercise 1: Find the Right Verb
Complete the following sentences by using the present tense for each of the five verbs in the preceding table.

1. He _____ a new car.

2. He _____ to work every day.

3. She _____ many phone calls.

4. We _____ going away.

5. A good student _____ his homework every night.

Exercise 2: Correct the Mistakes
Correct the following sentences. Cross out the misused verb. Write the correct verb in the blank space.

1. He gots _____ the flu.

2. The storms was _____ scary.

3. That girl do _____ hard work.

4. I is _____ tired tonight.

5. They goes _____ to the movies every week.

To check your answers, refer to the appendix.

Vocabulary Related to Illiteracy

Persons who make many grammatical errors in their spoken or written language are apt to be called illiterate. The following vocabulary word list will acquaint you with words that are related to illiteracy. The word *illiteracy* means a lack of education and may imply the inability to read or write.

Word	benighted, adj.
Pronunciation	be-night-ed
Definition	Ignorant; unenlightened

▶ *The Dark Ages was a benighted era of superstition and fear.*

Word	impercipient, adj.
Pronunciation	im-per-cip-i-ent
Definition	Imperceptive; unaware

▶ *He was impercipient of her obvious distress.*

Word	inerudite, adj.
Pronunciation	in-er-u-dite
Definition	Unlearned

▶ *The teacher was dismayed at the number of inerudite boys in her class.*

Word	nescience, n.
Pronunciation	nes-cience
Definition	Ignorance

▶ *He was appalled by the nescience of his coworkers.*

Word	unschooled, adj.
Pronunciation	un-school-ed
Definition	Uneducated

▶ *Her aim was to teach the unschooled children in her village.*

Exercise 3: Write, Say, Define

Read the list of words related to illiteracy. Write the words in your notebook. Study the pronunciation. Say the words. Write their definitions and indicate whether a word is a noun, a verb, or an adjective.

What You've Learned

This section focused on the present and past tenses of verbs that are almost indispensable to carry on a comprehensive conversation. At the same time, it may be that because these verbs are so widely used, their misuse is such a frequent occurrence. One purpose of this section was to call your attention to the possible misuse of these verbs, and the other goal was to lay the foundation for other, even more pronounced errors that are troubling to anyone who wishes to speak correctly.

The Trouble with Contractions

In our written and spoken language, there are many contractions. A contraction is the form of making one word out of two, or in some cases it is simply the shortening of a longer word. *Don't*, for example, is a contraction of the two words: *do not*. *Can't* is a shortening of the word *cannot*.

Ⓔ *Alert!*

> The word *ain't* is a contraction of *are not, is not,* and *am not*. Most linguists strongly disapprove of this word. It may be because it's a word that is mostly used by less educated people, in rural areas. Some consider *ain't* a vulgarism.

Problems arise when a speaker loses sight of the original words that were combined to make a particular contraction. *Don't* is not a contraction of *does not*, yet many people use *don't* as a third-person-singular verb, saying, for example, "He don't come here anymore" instead of "He <u>doesn't</u> come here anymore." This is but one example of how a contraction can be used inappropriately. Nevertheless, unless you're writing a literary work or a scholarly thesis, contractions are perfectly acceptable.

Exercise 4: Contraction Origins

Read the contractions in the left-hand column; then in the blank space, write the words that were combined to form the contraction. Example: Let's = let us.

1. I'm _____

2. you've _____

3. he's _____

4. isn't _____

5. doesn't _____

6. don't _____

7. can't _____

8. won't _____

9. you're _____

10. that'll _____

To check your answers, refer to the appendix.
Now here is our Contractions Vocabulary:

Word	cohesion, n.
Pronunciation	co-he-sion
Definition	The action of sticking something tightly together; a union

▶ *Glue was used to form a strong cohesion between the broken parts of the plate, mending it.*

Word	consolidate, v.
Pronunciation	con-sol-i-date
Definition	To bring together; to unite

▶ *We need to consolidate our incomes.*

Word	encompassment, n.
Pronunciation	en-com-pass-ment
Definition	The act of inclusion, of bringing into a circle

▶ *The brick wall served as an encompassment of his estate.*

Word	incorporate, v.
Pronunciation	in-cor-po-rate
Definition	To combine; to form one body

▶ *They decided to incorporate their holdings into one corporation.*

Word	integration, n.
Pronunciation	in-te-gra-tion
Definition	The act of bringing something into one

harmonious unit

▶ *The integration of all races and ethnic groups is a noble undertaking.*

Exercise 5: Read, Write, Define
Read the Contractions Vocabulary list. Write the words in your notebook. Study the pronunciation. Say the words. Write the definitions and indicate if a word is a noun, a verb, or an adjective.

What You've Learned
It is hoped that this section on contractions has increased your understanding of how contractions are formed and how they can be used. Your understanding of which words were combined to form a particular contraction can help you to

avoid common grammatical errors that occur when the origin of a contraction is overlooked.

The Dreaded Double Negative

Closely related to the misuse of verbs and contractions is the bugaboo of the double negative. In addressing the problem of double negatives, Norman Foerster and J. M. Steadman Jr., authors of *Writing and Thinking*, are indignantly blunt: "Only the illiterate are guilty of such gross double negatives, as: 'I didn't want to do nothing. They don't never come on time.'" These gentlemen are correct in pointing out these errors because the use of double negatives is indeed a prevailing problem.

 Fact

It may interest you to know that all of the examples of misused words that appear in this book were actually spoken by people appearing on TV programs. It's a sad commentary on our educational system that such a large segment of our population fails to speak correctly.

Negative words include the following: *no, not, nothing, never, didn't, don't, can't, nor.* A double negative occurs when two negative words are used in the same sentence or phrase.

Example: The sentence "I didn't say nothing," is a double negative because *didn't* and *nothing* are both negative words. Correctly the sentence should read, "I didn't say <u>anything</u>," or perhaps, "I said nothing."

Exercise 6: Common Double-Negative Sentences

Read the following sentences. Note the double negatives and any other grammatical errors that you recognize. Cross out the misused words. Write the correct words in the blank space.

1. I can't do it no how. _____

2. He don't know no better. _____

3. I don't got no money. _____

4. She won't never do it. _____

5. They don't know nothing. _____

To check your answers, refer to the appendix.
Here is the Negative-Word vocabulary:

Word	nonchalant, adj.
Pronunciation	non-cha-lant
Definition	Unconcerned; indifferent

▶ *His nonchalant attitude annoyed her.*

Word	noncommittal, adj.
Pronunciation	non-com-mit-tal
Definition	Unwilling to commit oneself to a particular view, course, or the like

▶ *She was very noncommittal when I invited her to the party.*

Word	noncompliance, n.
Pronunciation	non-com-pli-ance
Definition	Disobedience; refusal to follow rules.

▶ *It's difficult for parents to deal with teenage noncompliance.*

Word	nonentity, n.
Pronunciation	non-en-ti-ty
Definition	A thing or person of no importance

▶ *The boss treated his clerk like a nonentity.*

Word	nonfeasance, n.
Pronunciation	non-fea-sance
Definition	The failure to perform or do something that should be done; a duty

▶ *The general who failed to protect his troops was guilty of nonfeasance.*

Exercise 7: Read, Write, Define

Read the Negative-Word vocabulary list. Write the words in your notebook. Study the pronunciation. Say the words. Write the definitions and indicate if a word is a noun, a verb, or an adjective.

What You've Learned

This concludes your introduction to the grammatical error of what is known as the double negative. It may interest you to watch some of the TV shows such as *Oprah* and *Judge Judy* or similar talk shows for the purpose of listening to how the guests on these programs speak. Keep track of any mispronounced or misused words and phrases that you may hear. Evaluate your own speech and think how misspoken language could be improved.

Misunderstanding Lay, Lie, *and* Lie

No discussion of misused nouns and verbs would be complete without addressing the troubling confusion that appears to exist between the verbs *to lay* and *to lie*, and the word *lie*, which can be used as a noun or a verb.

We will begin with the verb *to lay*. Basically, it means "to place something somewhere." However, *to lay* can have many other denotations as well. The following examples will show you how the verb can be used correctly in different ways. For more definitions and usage, please refer to a large dictionary.

Example: *To Lay, Present Tense*
1. Lay the book on the table.
2. I'll lay fresh sheets on the bed.
3. Birds and reptiles lay eggs.
4. He is a layman, not a preacher. (In this sentence, the word *lay* is used as a noun.)

Example: *To Lay, Past Tense*
1. My hen laid an egg this morning.
2. He laid the book on a table.

Example: *To Lay, as a Participle*

1. My hens are laying many eggs.
2. There are religious sects that use the practice of "laying on" of hands.

Example: *To Lie (Recline), Present Tense*

1. I like to lie in the sun.
2. Let sleeping dogs lie.
3. Go lie down if you're tired.

Example: *To Lie (Recline), Past Tense*

1. The sick man lay in bed for three days.
2. The cat lay by the fire all night.

Example: *To Lie (Recline), as a Participle*

1. I was lying down when he came.
2. Your glove was lying on the floor.

Example: *To Lie (Tell a Falsehood), Present Tense*

1. Don't lie to me.
2. That's a lie. (Here, *lie* is used as a noun.)

Example: *To Lie (Tell a Falsehood), Past Tense*

1. He lied to me.
2. The man lied every time he spoke.

Example: *To Lie (Tell a Falsehood), as a Participle.*

1. He is always lying to me.
2. A lying person can't be trusted to tell the truth.

Exercise 8: Choose the Right Verb

Read the following sentences. Select the correct verb. Cross out the incorrect word.

1. (Lay, Lie) down, Fido.
2. He (lay, lied) in bed all day.
3. I was (lying, laying) on the sofa when the phone rang.

To check your answers, refer to the appendix.
Here is some useful *Lay, Lie,* and *Lie* Vocabulary:

Word	ballad, n
Pronunciation	bal-lad
Definition	A lay, a song, a poem

▶ *She sang an Irish ballad.*

Word	copulation, n.
Pronunciation	co-pu-la-tion
Definition	The sexual act

▶ *Some people consider copulations a carnal sin.*

Word	deception, n.
Pronunciation	de-cep-tion
Definition	The act of deceiving, of misleading; fraud

▶ *The con man's deception left her penniless.*

Word	emplacement, n.
Pronunciation	em-place-ment
Definition	A location, a position, a placement (e.g., laid)

▶ *The soldiers prepared an emplacement for their guns.*

Word	fabrication, n.
Pronunciation	fab-ri-ca-tion
Definition	A made-up story; an untruth

▶ *Her excuse was a fabrication that no one believed.*

Word	prevaricate, v.
Pronunciation	pre-var-i-cate
Definition	To lie; to tell a falsehood

▶ *A political candidate may prevaricate in an attempt to defeat his opponent.*

Word	prone, adj.
Pronunciation	prone
Definition	Lying face-down.

▶ *She slept in a prone position.*

Word	recline, v.
Pronunciation	re-cline
Definition	To lean back; to rest; to lie down.

u *Let him recline on this sofa.*

Word	recumbent, adj.
Pronunciation	re-cum-bent
Definition	Lying down

▶ *She stepped over her recumbent dog to go to the kitchen.*

Word	supine, adj.
Pronunciation	su-pine
Definition	Lying on one's back

▶ *The baby rolled over to a supine position.*

Exercise 9: Write, Say, Define

Read the *Lay*, *Lie*, and *Lie* Vocabulary list. Write the words in your notebook. Study the pronunciation. Say the words. Write the definitions and indicate whether a word is a noun, a verb, or an adjective.

 Essential

> The greatest misuse of the verbs *to lay* and *to lie* occurs when people confuse the past tense of *to lie*, which is *to lay*, with the present tense of the verb *to lay*. In giving a command to their dog to lie down, many people say, "Lay down," instead of using the correct present tense, "lie down."

What You've Learned

You have now completed the section that focused on the misuse of the verb *to lay*, its homophone *to lie* (to recline), and its twin *to lie* (to tell an untruth). If you or someone you know has been confused by these verbs, it is hoped that you now understand how to use them correctly.

Correct Speech

If you can avoid making the pronunciation and grammar mistakes that were discussed in this chapter as well as the ones highlighted in Chapters 2 and 3, then you will have made great strides in improving your language skills. Nevertheless, in order to use your increased vocabulary to your greatest advantage and to be able to speak in a formal situation like a knowledgeable individual, there are several other points of correct speech that must be addressed.

Specifically, you must pay attention to the following language errors: misuse of the words *than, these,* and *them, well* and *good,* and *like, as,* and *if.* Redundancy is another bad speech habit that weakens what a person is trying to convey. Redundancy refers to the use of too many, or unnecessary, similar words to express a thought. See the following examples:

1a. **Wrong:** You are older than me.
1b. **Right:** You are older than I. (Use a common-case pronoun because the phrase implies: You are older than I am old.)
2a. **Wrong:** I want them apples.
2b. **Right:** I want these (or those) apples.

1a. **Wrong:** He plays the piano good.
1b. **Right:** He is a good pianist, or he plays the piano well.
2a. **Wrong:** I feel good.
2b. **Right:** I feel well.

1. **Wrong:** He like said to me.
1a. **Right:** He said to me, or as he said to me.

Currently the word *like* is greatly overused by teenagers. It is used indiscriminately, serving no purpose in expressing their ideas.

1. **Right:** I like ice cream. In this sentence, the word *like* is used correctly as a verb.
2a. **Wrong:** If I was you, I would go.
2b. **Right:** If I were you, I would go.
3a. **Wrong:** If he was ready, he would go.
3b. **Right:** If he were ready, he would go.

Use the verb *were* whenever you're expressing a supposition using the word *if*.

1. **Wrong:** At this point in time. (This is wrong because it's a redundancy. In this sentence, point and time mean the same thing.)
1a. **Right:** At this point, or at this time.

If you take the time to pay attention to the right way of using the words in the given examples, you will add polish to your use of the English language.

Words of Wisdom

Now we will add five more important words to your new vocabulary. These words all indicate intelligence or wisdom:

Word	assiduous, adj.
Pronunciation	as-sid-u-ous
Definition	Diligent; persistent

▶ *He was an assiduous student.*

Word	cognition, n.
Pronunciation	cog-ni-tion
Definition	The process of knowing, understanding, learning

▶ *The process of cognition develops rapidly during the first two years of life.*

Word	erudite, adj.
Pronunciation	er-u-dite
Definition	Learned; well educated

▶ *The professor was known to be an erudite woman.*

Word	intelligentsia, n.
Pronunciation	in-tel-li-gent-si-a
Definition	A social class of educated intellectuals

▶ *The intelligentsia often plays a major role in promoting social and political change.*

Word	omniscience, n.
Pronunciation	om-nis-cience
Definition	The faculty of knowing everything; an attribute of God

▶ *Humans do not possess the power of omniscience.*

Final Review
Brain teasers and exercises will help you review your list of thirty new words.

Exercise 10: Review Word Play

Complete the words by filling in the blanks.

1. non _ _ _ _ _ y

2. non _ _ _ p _ i _ _ c e

3. nonf _ _ s _ n _ _

4. non _ o _ _ _ t _ _ l

5. nonc _ a _ a n _

Exercise 11: Word Play: True or False

Read the words and given definitions: Indicate if the definitions are true or false. Write *T* for true, *F* for false.

Word	Definition	T or F
assiduous	Lazy	_____
erudite	Educated	_____
omniscience	The faculty of knowing everything	_____
cognition	Machinery	_____
fabrication	Dressmaking	_____
prevaricate	To lie	_____
recumbent	Obese	_____
benighted	Unenlightened	_____
consolidate	Unite	_____
integration	Separation	_____

To check your answers, refer to the appendix.

Exercise 12: Word Play: Three Letters

Complete the words by filling in the first three letters.

1. _ _ _ dite

2. _ _ _ elligentsia

3. _ _ _ ercipient

4. _ _ _ cience

5. _ _ _ chooled

6. _ _ _ orporate

7. _ _ _ ulation

8. _ _ _ lad

9. _ _ _ line

10. _ _ _ ine

To check your answers, refer to the appendix.

Exercise 13: Find the Hidden Words

Read the following list of words. Write them in your notebook. Study each word, and write down at least ten hidden words that you can find in each of the words.

1. cohesion
2. deception
3. encompassment
4. emplacement
5. prone

With the completion of this chapter, you've now had the opportunity of acquiring 120 words. You have also been immersed in a fairly comprehensive review of basic, yet very important grammar etiquette (e.g., rules that govern the correct use of the English language). With these fundamentals out of the way, you can forge ahead at a comfortable pace. A glance at the table of contents will prepare you for what lies ahead.

Chapter 5
Personal Health and Medical Terminology

It is important to acquaint yourself with terminology that applies to the structure and components of your body, as well as to your personal health. For this reason the vocabulary list will include words pertaining to human physiology. It is equally beneficial to learn more about the language of medical specialties. Then, should the need arise, you'll be better prepared to find the right professional and the right treatment to restore you to good health.

You and Your Body

You are the one who is responsible for the upkeep of your body. It's the only one you have. Your body is an extremely complex, finely tuned, and yet remarkably efficient machine. Many of us take better care of our cars than we do our bodies. When something goes wrong with our automobile, we immediately take it to a mechanic. Most of us know exactly what the mechanic is talking about when he tells us that this part of the car needs replacement or adjustment. The question is how well do we know the physiological makeup of our bodies? When a physician uses a scientific term in reference to a possible ailment, is the word familiar? Do we understand what we are being told without asking for an explanation and feeling stupid? The aim of this chapter is to provide basic all-purpose health-related vocabulary.

Exercise 1: Find the Location

Study the body names in the left column. Find their location in the right-hand column. Show a line connecting the body-part word with its correct physical location.

1.	epiglottis	collarbone
2.	esophagus	ear
3.	Eustachian tube	chest
4.	clavicle	throat
5.	pectoral muscle	chest
6.	pituitary gland	kidney
7.	renal artery	brain
8.	sternum	chest

To check your answers, refer to the appendix or the following vocabulary list.

Word	clavicle, n.
Pronunciation	clav-i-cle
Location	collarbone

▶ *The clavicle connects the sternum with the shoulder blades.*

Word	epiglottis, n.
Pronunciation	ep-i-glot-tis
Location	throat

▶ *The function of the epiglottis is to close your windpipe when you swallow food.*

Word	esophagus, n.
Pronunciation	e-soph-a-gus
Location	throat, neck chest

▶ *When you swallow, food goes down the esophagus to your stomach.*

Word	Eustachian tube, n.
Pronunciation	eu-sta-chian tube
Location	ears

▶ *The Eustachian tube leads from an opening in the middle ear to a cavity at the back of the nose. Children who have frequent colds often develop middle-ear infections (otitis media) via the Eustachian tubes.*

Word	pectoral muscle, n.
Pronunciation	pec-to-ral muscle

Location	chest

▶ *Exercise can develop your pectoral muscles.*

Word	pituitary gland, n.
Pronunciation	pi-tu-i-tar-y gland
Location	left side of the head, under the brain

▶ *The pituitary gland excretes vital hormones affecting growth and other aspects of physiological functions.*

Word	sternum, n.
Pronunciation	ster-num
Location	breastbone

▶ *Upper ribs are attached to the sternum.*

Exercise 2: Write, Say, Define

Write the Body-Part Vocabulary in your notebook. Study the pronunciation. Say the words. Note their function and location in your body.

What You've Learned

This concludes a brief introduction to what may be less familiar body-part terms. It is assumed that most people are familiar with names and the approximate location of such organs as the intestines, heart, kidney, liver, lungs, stomach, and reproductive organs. The following sections will offer other anatomical information and terminology.

Fact

Many anatomical names have Greek or Latin origins. The word *esophagus* comes from a combination of two Greek words, *oisein*, meaning "to be going or to carry," and the word *phagien*, which means, "to eat." The Eustachian tubes are named after an Italian anatomist, Bartolommeo Eustachio, who died in 1547.

When Health Problems Happen

Even if your body generally functions with remarkable precision and dependability, just as with the best machine in the world, things occasionally go wrong. When a health problem arises, how well are you prepared to give your doctor a knowledgeable description of your symptoms? The following exercise will provide a chance to test your knowledge and perhaps learn some new words.

Exercise 3: Identify Your Ailment

Read the symptoms list on the left and draw lines connecting the symptoms to the appropriate medical term.

Symptoms	Medical Term
Diarrhea, vomiting	Vertigo
Dizziness	Asthma
Muscle weakness, joint stiffness, pain	Gastroenteritis
Skin rash	Polymyalgia rheumatica
Wheezing	Dermatitis

To check your answers, refer to the appendix or the following vocabulary list.

Word	asthma, n.
Pronunciation	asth-ma
Definition	Respiratory breathing problems; wheezing

▶ *An asthma attack requires immediate medical attention.*

Word	dermatitis, n.
Pronunciation	der-ma-ti-tis
Definition	A skin rash that may be caused by an allergic reaction to something in the environment

▶ *A chemical in a cleanser that Sally used gave her a case of dermatitis.*

Word	gastroenteritis, n.
Pronunciation	gas-tro-en-ter-i-tis
Definition	Stomach and intestinal distress caused by a virus (flu) or food poisoning

▶ *Tourists who travel to underdeveloped countries risk coming down with gastroenteritis.*

Word	Polymyalgia rheumatica, n.
Pronunciation	pol-y-my-al-gi-a rheu-mat-i-ca
Definition	A fairly common disease involving muscles and joints

▶ *Her polymyalgia rheumatica was treated with aspirin and steroids.*

Word	vertigo, n.
Pronunciation	ver-ti-go
Definition	Dizziness (Vertigo is not a disease; it is a symptom of any number of possible disorders. If the dizziness is constant and severe, a doctor should be consulted.)

▶ *Mary's vertigo was caused by a middle-ear infection that affected her sense of balance.*

Exercise 4: Write, Say, Define

Write the Health Problems Vocabulary in your notebook. Study the pronunciation. Say the words. Note what the terms mean in regard to your health.

Essential

> *Polymyalgia rheumatic* is a term that is also derived from a combination of Greek words; in Greek *poly* means many, or multiple; *myos* is a Greek word for muscles. Most doctors pronounce *polymyalgia* with a hard *g* like in the word *get*. The term *rheumatica* is from a Greek word, *rheumatismos*.

What You've Learned

Sometimes people tend to ignore the first symptoms of a potential health problem. There may be a number of reasons for this behavior. They are in denial and expect the symptom or illness to go away, and sometimes it does. They dislike doctors. They don't have a regular family physician. They don't have insurance or the money to pay for medical care.

The lack of insurance or money for medical care is a serious social problem; nevertheless, help is available to those who take the initiative to seek assistance. If a symptom or ill health persists without improvement for several days, a prudent person should seek medical advice. Delay may result in a worsening of a potentially serious condition.

Choosing the Right Practitioner

Medical science and technology are now so advanced that no one person could possibly have the knowledge or skill to treat effectively the myriads of disorders that may afflict your body. The answer to this dilemma is specialization. If you look in the Yellow Pages, you will find the names of physicians listed according to their expertise in a specific field of medicine. Some of the terms applied to a particular specialty may be familiar; others may not be. The following exercise will test your knowledge.

Exercise 5: Identify the Specialty

Read the following list of medical specialists. In the blank space, identify what you believe to be each one's specialty. For example, a urologist works with the prostate.

Title	Pronunciation	Specialty
cardiologist, n.	car-di-ol-o-gist	_____
dermatologist, n.	der-ma-tol-o-gist	_____
gynecologist, n.	gy-ne-col-o-gist	_____
internist, n.	in-ter-nist	_____
neurologist, n.	neu-rol-o-gist	_____
oncologist, n.	on-col-o-gist	_____
ophthalmolo-gist, n.	oph-thal-mol-o-gist	_____
orthopedic surgeon, n.	or-tho-pe-dic surgeon	_____
otorhinolaryngol-ogist, n.	o-to-rhi-no-lar-yn-gol-o-gist	_____
pediatrician, n.	pe-di-a-tri-cian	_____
podiatrist, n.	po-di-a-trist	_____

To check your answers, refer to the appendix.

Exercise 6: Write, Say, Define

If any of these medical titles were unfamiliar to you, write them in your notebook. Study the pronunciation. Say the words. Write the specialty next to the title.

What You've Learned

If it becomes necessary for you to seek the expertise of a specialist, it is possible that you'll be treated by more than one doctor. In many cases, such as a stroke, for example, you may be seen by a neurologist, a gastrointestinal surgeon if you should require a feeding tube, and other professional caregivers. Knowing all of these terms will prepare you for any situation.

Other Health Care Professionals

This section will familiarize you with medical terms that apply to practitioners other than medical doctors. These practitioners are specialized in their own field of health care and play an important role as team and support members when your specialists require their talent.

Exercise 7: Definitions: True or False?

Read the following words and the given definitions. Determine whether the definitions are true or false. Write *T* for true, *F* for false.

Word	Definition	T or F
aphasia	Loss of appetite	_____
audiologist	Evaluates hearing loss	_____
pathologist	Gives massages	_____
physiotherapist	Gives IQ tests	_____

To check your answers, refer to the appendix or the following vocabulary list.

Word	aphasia, n.
Pronunciation	a-pha-sia

Definition	A loss of speech

▶ *A head injury caused her aphasia.*

Word	audiologist, n.
Pronunciation	au-di-ol-o-gist
Definition	A specialist trained in evaluating hearing loss

▶ *An audiologist prescribed a hearing aid.*

Word	pathologist, n.
Pronunciation	pa-thol-o-gist
Definition	A scientist who studies and identifies diseases

▶ *The pathologist studied a tissue sample with care.*

Word	physiotherapist, n.
Pronunciation	phys-i-o-ther-a-pist
Definition	A specialist who deals with physical impairment

▶ *After his knee surgery, Jim was referred to a physiotherapist.*

Word	masseuse, n.
Pronunciation	ma-suz
Definition	A woman who uses massage to relieve muscular pain

▶ *After several sessions with a masseuse, Amy began to feel better.*

Exercise 8: Write, Say, Define

Write the Health Care Vocabulary in your notebook. Study the pronunciation. Say the words. Write the definition and indicate whether a word is a noun, a verb, or an adjective.

What You've Learned

As you conclude the section on health care professionals and the relevant vocabulary, it is hoped that you will continue familiarizing yourself with terms that may be new to you and that you will maintain a schedule of daily or at least weekly review of all the words you have learned so far. Memorization and study is a good exercise for your mind. The more you learn and retain, the more receptive your brain becomes to accumulating, storing, and using new information.

Understanding Diagnostic Tests

As it was mentioned earlier in this chapter, the great and rapid advances in medicine have produced a vast network of specialists. Along with the major growth in specialized medicine and technology, innovative techniques have resulted in the development of highly sophisticated tools for diagnostic testing. Specialized physicians use these diagnostic measures for preventive health checks of internal organs as well as a precise diagnostic tool for ascertaining a suspected disorder.

Cancer of the large intestine, for example, is the third most-common type of cancer. For this reason your doctor may urge you to have a diagnostic health check of your colon every few years after the age of fifty. Early detection of cancer or a precancerous condition guarantees complete recovery. Undetected colon cancer that is allowed to spread can become untreatable leading to an early death. Exercise 9 will test your knowledge of the most commonly used diagnostic procedures.

 Fact

> Our respiratory system consists of our nose, throat, and the trachea (windpipe). Deep in the chest the trachea divides into two main tubes that bring air into the lungs. These tubes are called bronchi. During a bronchoscopy a flexible diagnostic tube is passed into these air passageways. An inflammation within the bronchi is called bronchitis.

Exercise 9: Make the Right Match

Read the names of the following diagnostic tests and match them by drawing a line to the body part they are used to examine. Example: A colonoscopy is performed to examine the colon.

Diagnostic Test	Body Part
angiography	lungs
bronchoscopy	heart
cardiac catheterization	stomach
echography	blood vessels
endoscopy	internal organs

To check your answers, refer to the appendix or the following vocabulary list.

Word	angiography, n.
Pronunciation	an-gi-og-ra-phy
Definition	A diagnostic procedure for examining the interior of blood vessels

▶ *The angiography was a painless procedure.*

Word	bronchoscopy, n.
Pronunciation	bron-chos-copy
Definition	A procedure for examining the bronchi and lungs by means of a flexible, lighted tube that is passed through the nose or mouth into the chest cavity

▶ *Before being treated for a chronic cough, Jim underwent a bronchoscopy.*

Word	cardiac catheterization, n.
Pronunciation	car-di-ac cath-e-ter-i-za-tion
Definition	An angiography of the heart, in which a tube is passed through a vein into the heart in order to investigate the heart at work

▶ *The cardiac catheterization gave Ann a clean bill of health.*

Word	echography, n.
Pronunciation	e-chog-ra-phy
Definition	A diagnostic procedure that uses ultrasound waves to detect possible abnormalities in the body

▶ *An echography revealed the presence of a tumor.*

Word	endoscopy, n.
Pronunciation	en-dos-co-py
Definition	A procedure that examines the interior of the stomach by means of a flexible lighted tube

▶ *An endoscopy confirmed the doctor's opinion that his patient had an ulcer.*

Exercise 10: Write, Say, Define

Write the Diagnostic Test Vocabulary in your notebook. Study the pronunciation. Say the words. Write the definitions and indicate whether a word is a noun, a verb, or an adjective.

Specialists and Dental Care

The days when a blacksmith used a pair of pliers to yank out a cowboy's abscessed tooth are lost in history. Over the years, especially in the final decades of the last century, advances in dental science and technology have been as remarkable as those in other fields of medicine. In dentistry, as in medicine, there are specialists ready to treat oral problems that may be beyond the expertise of your family dentist. Exercise 11 will give you an opportunity to see how familiar you are with these dental specialties and the dental problems they treat.

Exercise 11: Definitions: True or False?

Read the following words and the given definition. Determine whether the definitions are true or false. Write a *T* for true, *F* for false.

Problem	Specialist	T or F
caries	Periodontist	_____
gingivitis	Family dentist	_____
malocclusion	Orthodontist	_____

To check your answers, refer to the appendix or the following vocabulary list.

Word	caries, n.
Pronunciation	car-ies
Definition	Tooth decay, which can be treated by your family dentist

▶ *It is important to repair caries as soon as they appear.*

Word	gingivitis, n.
Pronunciation	gin-gi-vi-tis
Definition	A gum disease that can become a more serious condition called periodontitis

▶ *Gingivitis should be treated by a periodontist.*

Word	malocclusion, n.
Pronunciation	mal-oc-clu-sion
Definition	A misalignment of teeth so that one is unable to bite or chew properly

▶ *Patients with malocclusion should see an orthodontist.*

Exercise 12: Write, Say, Define

Write the Dental Vocabulary words in your notebook. Study the pronunciation. Say the words. Write the definitions and indicate whether the word is a noun, a verb, or an adjective.

Final Review

Now it's time for a final review of your new vocabulary words. Word play and exercise will test what you have learned and affix this new knowledge more firmly in your mind.

Exercise 13: Complete the Words

Add letters to complete the following vocabulary words.

1. c a r _ _ _

2. g i n _ _ _ _ _ _ _

3. p e r i o _ _ _ _ _ _ _

4. o r t h o _ _ _ _ _ _ _

5. a p h _ _ i a

6. p a t h o _ _ _ _ _ _

7. e p i _ _ _ _ _ _ _

8. c l a _ _ _ l e

9. e s o p h _ _ _ _ _

To check your answers, refer to the appendix.

Exercise 14: Find the Letters

Add the missing letters to complete the following vocabulary words.

1. E___tacian tubes

2. p___uitary gland

3. r___al a___ery

4. s___rnum

5. p___toral

6. v___tigo

7. a___hma

8. g___troenteritis

9. d___matitis

10. e___oscopy

To check your answers, refer to the appendix.

Exercise 15: Find the Word

Write the scientific word that applies to the following definitions.

1. Teeth: m ___ ___ ___ ___ ___ ___ ___ ___ ___ ___ ___

2. Lungs: b ___ ___ ___ ___ ___ ___ ___ ___ ___ ___ ___

3. Blood vessels: a _ _ _ _ _ _ _ _ _ _ _

4. Heart: c _ _ _ _ _ _ _   c _ _ _ _ _ _ _ _ _ _ _ _ _

   _ _ _

5. Women's health: g _ _ _ _ _ _ _ _ _ _ _ _

To check your answers, refer to the appendix.

Exercise 16: Hidden Words
Write the following vocabulary words in your notebook. Find the hidden words in each of the "parent" words.

1. audiologist
2. physiotherapist
3. polymyalgia rheumatica
4. internist
5. echography

Chapter 6
Pregnancy, Childhood, and Parenting

The miracles of birth and parenthood are among the most exciting and fulfilling parts of human life. There is a lot of terminology that accompanies these subjects as well, and it's a good idea to be acquainted with it, whether you have children or even plan to have them in the future. This chapter focuses on the vocabulary of pregnancy and birth, childhood characteristics, and the experience of parenting.

Pregnancy and Birth

The birth of a baby changes the dynamics of a couple's relationship. No longer simply man and wife, or lovers, they are now parents. In this new role, they are responsible for the care and rearing of their child for the next eighteen to twenty-one years. From the moment of conception until your child's maturity, there may be many concerns that will have to be resolved. The vocabulary lists in this chapter will address some of these issues. Test your knowledge about pregnancy and birth with the following exercise.

 Essential

> As soon as a baby is born the doctor examines the neo-nate checking off five vital signs according to the Apgar Scale developed by Virginia Apgar in 1953. The Scale, a quick appraisal of the hear rate, respiration, muscle tone, reflex responsiveness, and skin color, gives a good indication of a baby's heath and future development.

Exercise 1: Complete or Define

Read the Pregnancy Vocabulary. Select one of the following words either to complete a two-word scientific name, or define a single-word term: *pregnancy, kidney inflammation, fluid, danger signal,* and *diagnostic procedure.*

1. amniotic _____
2. amniocentesis _____

3. eclampsia _____
4. ectopic _____
5. pyelitis _____

To check your answers, refer to the appendix or the following vocabulary list.

Word	amniotic fluid, n.
Pronunciation	am-ni-o-tic flu-id
Definition	A fluid that surrounds the developing fetus within a membrane sack inside the uterus

▶ *The amniotic fluid protects the fetus against injuries and fulfills other important functions.*

Word	amniocentesis, n.
Pronunciation	am-ni-o-cen-te-sis
Definition	A diagnostic procedure using a needle to withdraw amniotic fluid for analysis to determine whether the fetus has a genetic abnormality such as spina bifida, Down syndrome, or some other disorder

▶ *She eagerly awaited the results of the amniocentesis.*

Word	eclampsia, n.
Pronunciation	e-clamp-si-a
Definition	A serious condition involving kidney malfunction

▶ *Her swollen feet and high blood pressure indicated the onset of eclampsia.*

Word	ectopic pregnancy, n.
Pronunciation	ec-top-ic preg-nan-cy
Definition	A pregnancy occurring outside the uterus (When the fertilized egg fails to descend into the uterus and the fetus begins developing within a fallopian tube, the pregnancy has to be terminated.)

▶ *About one in two hundred pregnancies is ectopic. Severe abdominal pain can indicate this abnormality, which requires immediate medical attention.*

Word	pyelitis, n.
Pronunciation	py-e-li-tis
Definition	A kidney inflammation

▶ *Drinking several glasses of water daily can help to prevent pyelitis.*

Exercise 2: Write, Say, Define

Write the Pregnancy Vocabulary in your notebook. Study the pronunciation. Say the words. Write the definition and indicate whether a word is a noun, a verb, or an adjective.

Exercise 3: Birthing Vocabulary

Match the vocabulary words with the correct definition, drawing a line between the two words.

1. breech presentation   Baby appears face-up
2. cesarean section   Vaginal incision
3. episiotomy   Surgery

4. occipital presentation   Baby appears buttocks first
5. neonate   Newborn

To check your answers, refer to the appendix or the following vocabulary list.

Word	breech presentation, n.
Pronunciation	breech
Definition	Baby appears in a fetal position, buttocks first; may require a cesarean section delivery

Word	cesarean section, n.
Pronunciation	ce-sar-e-an
Definition	Surgical delivery of a baby through an incision in the abdomen and uterus

Word	episiotomy, n.
Pronunciation	e-pis-i-ot-o-my
Definition	Incision made to widen the vaginal opening during labor

▶ *The episiotomy hastened the baby's entrance into the world.*

Word	neonate, n.
Pronunciation	ne-o-nate
Definition	Newborn (The term is derived from the Greek word *neos* (new) and the Latin word *nasci* (born). An infant is called a neonate from the day of birth until the fourth week of life.)

Word	occipital presentation, n.
Pronunciation	oc-cip-i-tal
Definition	A presentation in which the baby enters the birth canal face-up (In a normal birth, the baby appears face-down.)

Exercise 4: Write, Say, Define

Write the Birthing Vocabulary in your notebook. Study the pronunciation. Say the word. Write the definition and indicate whether a word is a noun, a verb, or an adjective.

 Fact

Cesarean sections have been performed since ancient times, but back then, they were only done on dead or dying women. The first operation to be performed on a living woman was done by a Swiss butcher on his wife in 1500. The word *cesarean* may have been derived from the Latin verb *caedere*, to cut. However, the term has also been attributed to Julius Caesar who was reported to have been born in this manner.

A Child's Positive Characteristics

In this section your vocabulary will focus on words that describe children's desirable personality traits and behaviors. It is hoped that such a vocabulary will help parents recognize, praise, and encourage their child's exemplary character.

Exercise 5: Find the Antonyms

Study the Positive Characteristics Vocabulary in the left column. From the following antonyms (words that have an opposite meaning), select the appropriate antonym for the vocabulary words. The antonyms you may choose from are *unaware, delayed, selfish, lethargic, unimaginative.*

1. altruistic _____

2. innovative _____

3. perceptive _____

4. precocious _____

5. vivacious _____

To check your answers, refer to the appendix or the following vocabulary list.

Word	altruistic, adj.
Pronunciation	al-tru-is-tic
Definition	Unselfish; devoted to the well-being of humanity

▶ *Mother Teresa was an altruistic woman.*

Word	innovative, adj.
Pronunciation	in-no-va-tive
Definition	Creative, inventive, having new ideas

▶ *Famous fashion designers tend to be innovative.*

Word	perceptive, adj.
Pronunciation	per-cep-tive
Definition	Having an awareness or an ability to quickly understand, comprehend a situation

▶ *A perceptive child does well in school.*

Word	precocious, adj.
Pronunciation	pre-co-cious
Definition	Exhibiting early advanced development, especially mental

▶ *A precocious child, Nancy learned to read before she was three.*

Word	vivacious, adj.
Pronunciation	vi-va-cious
Definition	Lively in temperament and action

▶ *A vivacious child is usually a bright and healthy child.*

Exercise 6: Write, Say, Define

Write the positive characteristics in your notebook. Study the pronunciation. Say the words. Write the definition and indicate whether a word is a noun, a verb, or an adjective.

What You've Learned

It would be a mistake to attribute these positive characteristics only to children. Unless something particularly traumatic and damaging happens in childhood, early personality traits generally remain unchanged even as the child develops into adulthood. Thus, these words will be useful to you in various situations.

 Essential

It might be of interest to note that the word *altruistic* comes from the English word *altruism*, which in turn comes from the French word *altruisme*. Originally, it appears that the French expression *altruisme* was derived from the Italian term *altrui*. In any language altruism is the opposite of egoism.

A Child's Negative Characteristics

No one is perfect. The most charming, obedient, and delightful child may at times display negative attitudes or behavior. It is therefore necessary to include vocabulary words that describe less desirable personality traits. It's also helpful to remember that when everything that a child says or does is consistently negative, the behavior may be a symptom of maladjustment to a home or school situation rather that an inborn personality deficit. In such a case, wise and loving parents seek the professional advice of a child psychologist.

Exercise 7: Find the Antonyms

Study the Negative Characteristics Vocabulary in the left column. From the following antonyms (words that have an opposite meaning), select the appropriate antonym for the vocabulary words. You may choose from these antonyms: *happy, quiet, energetic, agreeable, stable.*

1. capricious _____

2. contentious _____

3. lachrymose _____

4. lethargic _____

5. obstreperous _____

To check your answers, refer to the appendix or the following vocabulary list.

Word	capricious, adj.
Pronunciation	ca-pri-cious
Definition	Changeable; motivated by mood swings

▶ *Betsy's capricious behavior was a bid for her father's attention.*

Word	contentious, adj.
Pronunciation	con-ten-tious
Definition	Argumentative; quarrelsome

▶ *John's contentious attitude alienated his classmates.*

Word	lachrymose, adj.
Pronunciation	lach-ry-mose
Definition	Tearful

▶ *Softhearted Susie was a lachrymose child.*

Word	lethargic, adj.
Pronunciation	le-thar-gic
Definition	Sluggish; sleepy; slow-moving

▶ *Children who don't get enough sleep tend to be lethargic in school.*

Word	obstreperous, adj.
Pronunciation	ob-strep-er-ous
Definition	Noisy; unruly; resisting control

▶ *The teacher was unable to control the obstreperous boys in her class.*

 Fact

Like many other terms, the words *lachrymus* and *obstreperus* have Latin roots. The Latin word *lacrimosis* is derived from the word *lacrima,* which means a tear. *Obstreperus* is spelled in Latin closely to the way that it's spelled in English; *obstreperous,* meaning, clamorous and/or boisterous.

Exercise 8: Write, Say, Define

Write the Negative Characteristics Vocabulary in your notebook. Study the pronunciation. Say the words. Write the definition; indicate whether a word is a noun, a verb, or an adjective.

Exercise 9: Use the Words

If you are a parent or someone who is frequently in contact with children, observe their actions and personality traits. Do any of the positive and negative vocabulary words apply to their behaviors and interactions with each other? Are any of these words descriptive of people you encounter at work, at home, or in social situations?

Negative Parenting Styles

Many factors influence the parenting style that individuals adopt in rearing their young. First-time parents are generally complete novices regarding the skills of successful parenthood. All they know about how to raise a child is based upon their own childhood experiences and their own relationships with their parents. If their childhood was a happy one, if they were guided by loving yet responsible adults who set reasonable limits, but never treated their children harshly or unjustly, then as adults these individuals might be expected to use the same approach in caring for their own young. Nevertheless, there are other factors, such as the background of the other parent, that come into play. There may be cultural factors as well as differences in personality traits, personal goals, and expectations for their child. Individual life experiences, level of education, and the degree of harmony in the marital relationship can also influence how a child is raised. The vocabulary in this section consists of words that describe what could be considered negative parenting styles. Negative parenting implies an approach that hampers a child's potential for optimal mental, emotional, and personality development. Parents don't necessarily deliberately adopt negative parenting styles, and they are usually completely unaware of how their behavior is affecting their children. What they do as parents may be done through ignorance or through the influence of outside factors; they raise their children in a manner that reflects their own needs and beliefs.

 Essential

The term laissez-faire comes from the French meaning to allow to act. As a parenting style it's called permissiveness. Permissive parents choose to ignore a child's inappropriate behaviors. The demands of child rearing—guiding and setting limits—are simply too overwhelming for some individuals. They don't trust themselves to do the right thing. It's easier to do nothing. This is another example of parental insecurity. Children from laissez-faire households may become underachievers and troublemakers in school.

Exercise 10: Find the Antonyms

Study the Negative Parenting Styles words in the left column. From the following antonyms (words that have an opposite meaning), select the appropriate antonym for the vocabulary terms. You may choose from the following antonyms: *egalitarian, altruistic, involved, open-minded, tolerant, cheerful.*

1. autocratic   _____

2. egocentric   _____

3. inflexible   _____

4. laissez-faire   _____

5. morose   _____

To check your answers, refer to the appendix or the following vocabulary list.

Word	autocratic, adj.
Pronunciation	au-to-crat-ic
Definition	Dictatorial; domineering; trying to be in absolute control

▶ *A child raised by autocratic parents may eventually rebel.*

Word	egocentric, adj.
Pronunciation	e-go-cen-tric
Definition	Selfish; regarding oneself as the center of all things

▶ *A celebrity may become egocentric and neglectful of others.*

Word	inflexible, adj.
Pronunciation	in-flex-i-ble
Definition	Rigid; unwilling to negotiate or compromise

▶ *Inflexible parents alienate their children.*

Word	laissez-faire, adj.
Pronunciation	lais-sez-faire

Definition	Exhibiting a policy of noninterference, noninvolvement, or indifference

▶ *A laissez-faire attitude toward children leaves a child bereft of guidance and parental attention.*

Word	morose, adj.
Pronunciation	mo-rose
Definition	Sullen; gloomy

▶ *A morose individual brings little happiness into a home.*

Exercise 11: Write, Say, Define

Write the Negative Parenting Styles vocabulary in your notebook. Study the pronunciation. Say the words. Write the definitions and indicate whether a word is a noun, a verb, or an adjective.

Positive Parenting Styles

It is quite possible that persons who adopt a positive parenting style are individuals who had a happy childhood. Through adulthood, they maintain warm and comfortable relationships with their parents. As a result, they follow in their parents' footsteps, emulating their mother's and father's styles in dealing with their own children. This, however, is not always the case. Sometimes, adults who came from unhappy, dysfunctional homes are mature enough to discard the injustices and unhappiness they may have experienced as children and vow never to repeat their parents' misguided and sometimes severely damaging behavior toward their young. As you turn to Exercise 12, you can see how familiar you are with words that describe desirable parenting styles.

Exercise 12: Find the Antonym

Study the Positive Parenting Styles words in the left column. From the following antonyms (words that have an opposite meaning), select appropriate antonyms for the vocabulary terms. You may choose from the following antonyms: *alienation, indifference, impatience, negligence.*

1. affinity   _____

2. cynosure   _____

3. empathy   _____

4. forbearance _____

To check your answers, refer to the appendix or the following vocabulary list.

Word	affinity, n.
Pronunciation	af-fin-i-ty
Definition	A natural attraction, mutual affection, or closeness

▶*The affinity between the children and their parents was obvious.*

Word	cynosure, n
Pronunciation	cyn-o-sure
Definition	An object that guides by example

▶*She used cynosure as a method to teach her children good manners.*

Word	empathy, n.
Pronunciation	em-pa-thy
Definition	The ability to understand or to sense the feelings of another person or animal

▶*The boy appreciated his father's empathy when his team lost a game.*

Word	forbearance, n.
Pronunciation	for-bear-ance
Definition	Patience; tolerance and restraint

▶ *Lucy's mother showed forbearance when the girl laughed noisily with her friends.*

Exercise 13: Write, Say, Define

Write the Positive Parenting Styles in your notebook. Study the pronunciation. Say the words. Write the definition and indicate whether a word is a noun, a verb, or an adjective.

What You've Learned

This brings you to the end of the section that acquainted you with a vocabulary that describes what are considered positive parenting styles. These words reflect attitudes and child-rearing practices that are the most conductive to raising happy, well-adjusted children who, as research has shown, are able to grow up to be successful, self-confident adults.

Final Review

Exercise 14: Complete the Words

Read the following list and add the missing letters to complete the words.

1. e c t o _ _ _

2. n e o _ _ _ _

3. a m n _ _ _ _ _ _ fluid

4. e p i s i o _ _ _ _

5. a m n i o _ _ _ _ _ _ _ _ _

6. o c c i _ _ _ _ _ presentation

7. p y e _ _ _ _ _

8. e c l a m _ _ _ _

9. b r e _ _ _ presentation

Exercise 15: Find the Missing Letters

Study the following and fill in the missing letters to complete the words.

1. a l _ _ u i _ _ _ c

2. i _ n _ v _ t _ v _

3. _ _ r c _ _ t _ v _

4. p _ e c _ c _ o _ _

5. v _ v _ c _ _ _ s

6. c _ n t _ n _ _ _ _ s

7. o b _ _ r _ p _ _ o _ s

8. l e _ _ a _ g _ c

9. _ a c _ _ y _ o _ e

10. c a _ _ i _ i _ u _

Exercise 16: Find the Right Word

Read the definitions in the left column and write the vocabulary words in the provided space.

1. dictatorial _____

2. self-centered _____

3. permissive _____

4. gloomy _____

5. natural attraction _____

6. insight, compassion _____

7. tolerance _____

8. setting an example,
   guidance _____

To check your answers, refer to the appendix.

Chapter 7
The Universe: Scientific Terminology

The word *universe* comes from the Latin word *universus*, meaning the "entire whole." As it is used today, *universe* is defined as the whole body of things and phenomena that are observed and postulated. Earth, the sky, the oceans, and every plant and living organism are a part of this immense, mysterious entity, which goes beyond our sight, comprehension, and at this point, exploration. In striving to understand these mysteries, humans have created a large vocabulary on this topic.

Star Gazing

As ancient scholars, prophets, and seers studied the heavens, they made discoveries and formed conclusions; some were right but many of their theories were later proved wrong. We are still seeking answers, although such great strides have been made in the field of astronomy that it boggles the mind to think of what may be learned and attained in the future. In this section, you will study words related to astronomy. Very likely, some of the words are familiar to you, yet you may not know their exact definitions. The following exercise will test your knowledge.

 Fact

> Greek astronomers observed that some celestial bodies that we call stars remained fixed in place, while others were in motion. We call these moving celestial bodies planets from the Greek word *planes,* meaning wanderer. Planets are not self-illuminating. Their light comes from the sun. Eight planets orbit the sun; in order of their closeness to the sun they are Mercury, Venus, Earth, Jupiter, Saturn, Uranus, Neptune, and Pluto.

Exercise 1: Definitions: True or False?

Read the following list of Astronomical Terms and the given definitions. Determine if a definition is true or false. Write *T* for true, *F* for false.

Word	Definition	T or F
ascension	The rising of a celestial body	_____
asteroid	A star	_____
celestial	Angelic , heavenly	_____
cerulean	Sky-blue	_____
constellation	A group of stars	_____
equinox	The first day of winter	_____
meridian	A body of water	_____
moon	Revolves around the sun	_____
planetarium	The study of astrology	_____
satellite	An orbiting celestial body	_____

To check your answers, refer to the appendix or the following vocabulary list.

Word	ascension, n.
Pronunciation	as-cen-sion
Definition	The rising of a celestial body (e.g., the sun)

▶ *They awaited the sun's ascension.*

Word	asteroid, n.
Pronunciation	as-ter-oid
Definition	One of thousands of small planets chiefly between Mars and Jupiter.

▶ *An asteroid isn't likely to hit Earth.*

Word	celestial, adj.
Pronunciation	ce-les-ti-al
Definition	Heavenly

▶ *The moon is a celestial body.*

Word	cerulean, adj.
Pronunciation	ce-ru-le-an
Definition	Sky-blue

▶ *They gazed at the clear, cerulean sky.*

Word	constellation, n.
Pronunciation	con-stel-la-tion
Definition	A group or formation of stars

▶ *The Big Dipper is a constellation.*

Word	equinox, n.
Pronunciation	e-qui-nox
Definition	A biannual event when the sun crosses the equator and the length of day and night is equal all over the world

▶ *The vernal (spring) equinox usually occurs on March 21.*

Word	meridian, n.
Pronunciation	meri-dian
Definition	A great imaginary circle on Earth's surface that passes through the North and South poles and at any place between

▶ *Astronomers use the meridian line to chart the location of stars.*

Word	moon, n.
Pronunciation	moon

| Definition | A satellite that revolves around Earth, shining by the sun's reflected light |

▶ *The planet Jupiter has four large moons and many smaller ones.*

Word	planetarium, n.
Pronunciation	plan-e-tar-i-um
Definition	An apparatus or model representing the planetary system

▶ *The planetarium was housed in a building with a domed ceiling.*

Word	satellite, n.
Pronunciation	sat-el-lite
Definition	A celestial body that orbits a larger one

▶ *In astronomy, celestial satellites are called moons.*

Exercise 2: Write, Say, Define

Write the Astronomical Terms vocabulary in your notebook. Study the pronunciation. Say the words. Write the definitions and indicate whether a word is a noun, a verb, or an adjective.

What You've Learned

Astronomy is a fascinating science. On a clear night as we gaze at a midnight sky where innumerable stars cast their brilliance, we are filled with awe and wonder. For thousands of years, humans have studied the heavens, probing its mysteries. But the universe is a mystery itself. In the heavens and within Earth, there are questions to be answered, discoveries to be made. Scientists in every imaginable field are constantly at work seeking and acquiring new knowledge. In the next section, your vocabulary will be related to the sciences of archeology, geology, paleontology, and paleobotany.

 Essential

Today, astrology is a pseudoscience that deals with the influence of stars upon human affairs and the foretelling of future events. In ancient Greece and Rome astrology had the meaning of astronomy. In early times when it was believed that Earth was the center of the universe, it was not surprising that people assumed that the "wandering" planets might influence their destiny and human behavior.

Digging Deep

Beneath the ground upon which we walk, build our homes, and plant our crops are buried secrets of the universe and of life on our planet that go back millions of years. Four main fields of scientific discovery dig deep into the soil to uncover what lies hidden, buried by the eons. These four disciplines are archeology, geology, paleontology, and paleobotany. *Archeology*, sometimes spelled *archaeology*, originates from the Greek word *arche*, meaning "beginning" and implying something very old. Archeologists focus on the study of human evolution from prehistoric times to the present. By systematic excavation, archeologists discover, collect, and analyze relics, crude stone tools, pottery, and other artifacts that tell the history of our distant ancestors. *Geology* comes from the Greek word *ge*, which means "earth, ground, or soil." This is a science that deals with the history of the earth, of rock formations, and of mineral deposits. Today geology is a complex field of study and research that ranges from monitoring earthquakes and volcanoes to mining and drilling for oil. The third science that is concerned with the historic past of our planet is paleontology. The term comes from the Greek words *palatios*, "ancient," and *onta*, "existing." This science deals mainly with fossil remains: the bones and skeletons of extinct animals. Paleobotany is a branch of botany that deals with fossil plants.

Here is a list of some scientific terms:

Word	artifact, n.
Pronunciation	ar-ti-fact
Definition	Any object or ornament produced by humans

▶ *Archeologists seek prehistoric artifacts.*

Word	eolith, n.
Pronunciation	e-o-lith
Definition	A crudely chipped stone artifact, such as a flint, from the beginning of human culture

▶ *An eolith indicates a human being's first attempt at making a tool out of stone.*

Word	fossil, n.
Pronunciation	fos-sil
Definition	An ancient preserved impression or remain of a plant or animal

▶ *Dinosaur bones and skeletons are fossils.*

Word	*Homo sapiens*, n.
Pronunciation	Homo sa-pi-ens
Definition	The modern species of humans

▶ *The term* Homo sapiens *comes from the New Latin;* homo *means "man," and* sapiens *means "wise, intelligent"; hence, the two-word term.*

Word	Paleolithic Period, n.
Pronunciation	Pa-le-o-lith-ic Pe-ri-od
Definition	Also known as the Old Stone Age; a subdivision of the Stone Age

▶ *Neanderthal and the Cro-Magnon early humans belonged to the Paleolithic Period.*

Word	Neolithic Period, n.
Pronunciation	Ne-o-lith-ic Pe-ri-od
Definition	Cultural period characterized by polished stone implements, pottery, and primitive spinning and weaving

▶ *During the Neolithic Period, humans were learning new skills including agriculture.*

Word	Stone Age, n.
Pronunciation	Stone Age

Definition   The earliest known period of human
               culture, when humans began creating
               stone tools and weapons

▶ *At the beginning of Stone Age, stone tools and weapons were crudely made.*

ⓔ *Fact*

The Neanderthal man is named for the Neander Valley in Germany where the first skeletal remains of this species were found. Neanderthals are regarded as a race of cave dwellers who preceded modern man. Cro-Magnons were a race of tall erect men who belong to the same species as *Homo sapiens*, i.e., modern man. Cro-Magnon remains were discovered in France and were named after the cave where they were found.

Exercise 3: Write, Say, Define

Write the Scientific Terms vocabulary in your notebook. Study the pronunciations. Say the words. Write the definitions and indicate whether the word is a noun, a verb, or an adjective.

What You've Learned

There is still much hidden from our view. Our universe likes to keep its secrets, tantalizing inquisitive minds to continue their search for more knowledge about the past, the present, and the future. In the following section, words relating to the immensity of our oceans and seas and what lies beneath their calm or turbulent waves will be added to your vocabulary.

Beneath the Sea

Oceans and seas cover approximately 70 percent of Earth's surface. The vastness, the depth, and the power of these waters are almost beyond human comprehension. Glittering like gold in the sunlight or shimmering like silver under the moonlight, we are mesmerized by the oceans' beauty. At times, we also flee in terror from the devastation of a tidal wave. The oceans teem with living plants and sea creatures, ranging from enormous mammals such as whales to microscopic organisms. The sciences of oceanography and marine biology are dedicated to studying the dynamics of the oceans and all that is hidden beneath their waves. Your new vocabulary will focus on scientific terms relating to the study of our oceans and seas.

 Essential

> According to Greek mythology, Medusa was one of three Gorgon sisters who had snakes for hair and were so horrible that anyone who saw them would turn into stone. The Portuguese man-of-war is another strange name for a large species of jellyfish. In Japan jellyfish are cut into thin strips, cooked, and served as noodles. These jellyfish noodles, however, are very tough to chew.

Here is some Marine Biology Vocabulary:

Word	benthology, n.
Pronunciation	ben-thol-o-gy
Definition	The study of organisms at the bottom of the sea

▶ *Marine biologists engage in benthology.*

Word	echinoderm, n.
Pronunciation	e-chi-no-derm
Definition	Any marine animal with prickly skin, such as a starfish or sea urchin, that is radially symmetrical

▶ Echinoderm *comes from the Greek words* echin, *"prickly," and* derma, *"skin."*

Word	medusa, n.
Pronunciation	me-du-sa
Definition	A jellyfish

▶ Medusa *is a name from Greek mythology.*

Word	plankton, n.
Pronunciation	plank-ton
Definition	Minute organisms found in the oceans and other bodies of water

▶ *Various sea animals feed on plankton.*

Word	thermocline, n.
Pronunciation	ther-mo-cline

Definition   A temperature zone in a body of water that represents the transition in temperature between the surface layer and the deeper layer

▶ *Thermocline is the layer of water that separates the warmer, upper, oxygen-rich zone of a lake or sea from the lower, colder, oxygen-poor zone.*

Exercise 4: Write, Say, Define
Refer back to the Marine Biology Vocabulary. Write the words. Study the pronunciations. Say the words. Write the definitions and indicate whether the word is a noun, a verb, or an adjective.

The Invisible World

Inhabitants of the invisible part of our world are all around us. They may be in the air we breathe, in the water we drink, or in the soil we dig. They live on plants and animals, in our food, and on things we touch. They are commonly called germs or microbes. Scientifically, they are known as microorganisms, living entities that cannot be seen without a microscope. Medically, some of these microorganisms are designated as infectious agents. The two major agents that can cause disease are viruses and bacteria. Antibiotics cannot control viruses. Their danger and power lie in the fact that they invade living cells where the viruses grow and multiply. The only protection against them is a viral vaccine. Another problem is that viruses change and mutate. As a result, new vaccines must be developed to combat new viruses.

Most of us are aware that influenza, the flu, is caused by a virus. Health-conscious individuals routinely get flu shots to avoid contracting the illness. The flu virus is airborne and very contagious. Coughing and sneezing can spread the disease.

Bacteria exist all around us. Some bacteria are harmless; others cause various sicknesses. Since bacterial infections can be cured with antibiotics, many ailments are less life-threatening than they were in the past. Refer to Exercise 5 to test your knowledge of this invisible world of microorganisms.

Exercise 5: True or False?
Read the sentences and indicate whether they are true or false. Write *T* for true, *F* for false.

1. Antibiotics can cure a cold. _____

2. Leprosy is caused by bacteria. _____

3. A vaccine can prevent rabies in animals. _____

4. A virus, herpes simplex, causes cold sores. _____

5. Ticks and mosquitoes can carry infectious diseases. _____

To check your answers, refer to the appendix.

Here is a list of more Invisible World Vocabulary:

Word	immunize, v.
Pronunciation	im-mu-nize
Definition	To protect from disease by the use of a vaccine or other method

▶ *It is important to immunize infants against diphtheria and other childhood diseases.*

Word	microbiology, n.
Pronunciation	mi-cro-bi-ol-o-gy
Definition	The science that deals with microorganisms

▶ *Researchers in microbiology have made significant scientific and medical discoveries.*

Word	staphylococcus, n.
Pronunciation	staph-y-lo-coc-cus
Definition	A harmless bacterium unless it enters the body through a wound or injury, in which case it can cause serious illness

▶ *A diabetic can be susceptible to severe staphylococcus infections.*

Word	streptococcus, n.
Pronunciation	strep-to-coc-cus
Definition	A species of bacteria that can cause serious illness

▶ *A streptococcus infection can cause pneumonia.*

Exercise 6: Write, Say, Define

Write the Invisible World Vocabulary in your notebook. Study the pronunciations. Say the words. Write the definitions and indicate whether the word is a noun, a verb, or an adjective.

Alert!

In addition to the viruses and bacteria that inhabit the invisible world, there are several fungi and parasites that can make us ill. There are fungi that can infect the lungs when we happen to inhale fungus spores (seeds) that are airborne. Parasites are organisms that invade our bodies. Tapeworm, for example, can be passed on to humans through inadequately cooked tapeworm-infested pork, beef, or fish. A more deadly parasite that causes trichinosis can be found in pork and beef.

What You've Learned

Although we are surrounded by myriad unseen, potentially dangerous microorganisms, do not panic. If you use common sense and follow the rules of good hygiene, you need not be concerned. Should you become ill, rely on ever-expanding medical technology to make you well again.

Clouds and Weather

To quote Mark Twain: "Everybody talks about the weather, but no one does anything about it." Well, we still talk about the weather and still can't do anything about changing it, but we know a great deal more about it than in Mark Twain's time. Our meteorologist can tell us what to expect. Orbiting weather satellites circling high above the clouds send minute-by-minute data back to Earth. Meteorologists on weather channels and news programs use charts, figures, and photographs to analyze, predict, alert, and prepare us for any weather-related emergency that might arise. They show us various cloud formulations. Clouds, which are masses of vapor that consist of tiny drops of water or ice crystals, play a significant role in determining weather conditions. Your Weather Vocabulary will name some of the most commonly seen clouds.

Name	cirrus, n.
Pronunciation	cir-rus
Definition	A white, wispy cloud

▶ *The cirrus cloud floated across the sky in a feather-shaped band.*

Name	cumulus, n.
Pronunciation	cu-mu-lus
Definition	Massive, dense clouds, seen in fair weather

▶ *Against the azure sky, the white cumulus clouds looked like mounds of whipped cream on a blue plate.*

Name	thundercloud, n.
Pronunciation	thun-der-cloud

| Definition | A dark massive cloud charged with electricity |

▶ *The thunderclouds massing over the mountains heralded a thunderstorm.*

Name	vapor, n.
Pronunciation	va-por
Definition	A visible hazy substance, such as steam or fog, floating in the air

▶ *A cloud is a mass of visible vapor.*

Exercise 7: Write, Say, Define

Write the Weather Vocabulary in your notebook. Study the pronunciations. Say the words. Write the definitions and indicate whether the word is a noun, a verb, or an adjective.

Final Review

The following review exercises will refresh your memory and help you to retain words that may not have been part of your conversational vocabulary.

Exercise 8: Find the Vowels

Complete the following list of words by inserting the missing vowels: *a, e, i, o, u.*

1. __ s c __ n s __ __ n

2. __ s t __ r __ __ d

3. c _ l _ st _ _ l

4. c _ r _ l _ _ n

5. c _ nst _ ll _ t _ _ n

6. _ q _ _ n _ x

7. m _ r _ d _ _ _ n

8. m _ _ n

9. pl _ n _ t _ r _ _ m

10. s _ t _ ll _ t _

Exercise 9: Complete the Words

Complete the following list of words by adding the last three letters.

1. artif _ _ _

2. eol _ _ _

3. fos _ _ _

4. Homo Sapi _ _ _

5. Stone _ _ _

6. Paleolit _ _ _   Age

7. Neolit _ _ _   Age

Exercise 10: Missing Letters

Complete the following list of words by supplying the missing letters.

1. b _ n _ _ o _ o _ y

2. _ c h _ n o d _ _ m

3. m _ _ u _ a

4. _ l a _ k _ o _

5. _ h e _ m _ c _ i _ e

6. i m _ u n _ z _ w

7. m _ c _ _ b _ _ l _ g _

8. s t _ p h _ l o _ o c c _ s

9. _ t r _ p _ o _ o c c _ s

Exercise 11: Write the Word

Read the given definition; write the defined word.

1. A wispy cloud   _____

2. A large cloud seen in fair weather _____

3. A storm cloud   _____

4. Steam or a hazy substance   _____

Chapter 8
The Law and Legal Terms

Without rules, and the ability to enforce them and to levy a consequence should a law be disobeyed, laws would be ineffectual and chaos would prevail. In today's complex society, there are innumerable laws laid down by the governing authority of a community, state, or nation that affect every aspect of our lives. In this chapter, you will find legal terms that apply to various circumstances that may require professional legal assistance.

Marriage and Children

Marriage is a legal binding contract between you and your spouse. The contract, a marriage certificate, gives you certain rights and responsibilities that are defined, regulated, and enforced by the state. A married couple may not devise their own rules; they must obey the law and that is not negotiable. For example, a child may not be adopted legally without due process. The law does not recognize the termination of a marriage without a divorce decree granted by the state. A marriage contract gives you the right to share a home and property, to have sex and raise your children, and to live outside of parental control. One may smile at some of these rights that a marriage certificate grants you. Regardless of what the law states, people have sex before marriage, and a married couple is not always free from interfering in-laws.

 Fact

A separation agreement is a binding document that lists, in detail, the rights and obligations of the involved individuals. Provisions are made for the division of property, the custody and support of children, payment of debts, as well as the question of inheritance should one of the spouses die. The separation contract is similar to a divorce decree except that a separated couple may not remarry without divorce.

Generally once a marriage contract is signed, the law does not interfere in the lives of the married couple as long as they fulfill their obligation to live as responsible individuals who are employed, who pay their bills, and who treat each other and their children with love and respect. Sadly, however, there are many instances when the law must step in to stop domestic violence, child neglect, abuse, and other dysfunctional family issues. The legal terms in this chapter will apply to situations that may require legal assistance as well as instances in which state or county authorities intervene because an unlawful or criminal act has been committed.

Here is a list of Family-Related Words:

Word	abandonment, n.
Pronounciation	a-ban-don-ment
Definition	The act of deserting or walking away from a person or property

▶ *The abandonment of a child is a crime punishable by law.*

Word	adultery, n.
Pronounciation	a-dul-ter-y
Definition	Voluntary sexual intercourse by a married person outside his or her marriage

▶ *Adultery is grounds for divorce.*

Word	alimony, n.
Pronounciation	al-i-mo-ny
Definition	Money paid by one spouse to an ex-spouse by order of a judge

▶ *The term* alimony *is gradually being replaced by the terms* maintenance *and* support.

Word	annulment, n.
Pronounciation	an-nul-ment
Definition	A court or church order stating that a marriage never existed

▶ *When Betty learned that her husband lied about his felonious past, she was granted an annulment.*

Word	bigamy, n.
Pronounciation	big-a-my
Definition	The crime of marrying someone while still married to another

▶ *Men who commit bigamy lead a double life. Bigamy is a crime punishable by law.*

Word	custody, n.
Pronounciation	cus-to-dy
Definition	Legally, the responsibility of keeping and caring for a person or property; legal confinement, such as protective custody of a person, as well as arrest and imprisonment

▶ *If a divorcing couple has children, a judge rules on which parent gets primary custody of the children.*

Word	prenuptial agreement, n.
Pronounciation	pre-nup-tial agree-ment

Definition	A contract between two people who plan to get married that spells out how their property would be divided in case of a divorce or the death of the spouse

▶ *A prenuptial agreement can forestall disputes and lawsuits, especially if there are children from previous marriages.*

Word	separation, n.
Pronounciation	sep-a-ra-tion
Definition	A legal agreement between married couples who no longer want to live together but are not divorced

▶ *A legal separation agreement allows a husband and a wife to lead independent lives.*

Exercise 1: Write, Say, Define

Write the Family-Related Words in your notebook. Study the pronunciation. Say the words. Write the definitions and indicate whether a word is a noun, a verb, or an adjective.

Money Matters

There are many federal and state laws governing businesses and financial institutions. As a private citizen, however, as long as you manage your finances legally, the law will not interfere with how you handle your money. Nevertheless, there are obligations that you must fulfill if you wish to stay out of trouble. As a responsible individual, you must pay taxes. If you own a house, you must pay a property tax. Once a year, you must pay income tax.

If you have a mortgage or you buy furniture and a car on credit, you must make installment payments on time. The legal terms in this section will relate to money, property, and the behaviors that can get you in trouble.

Word	abscond, v.
Pronounciation	ab-scond
Definition	To run away, escape with stolen money or valuables

▶ *The old woman feared that her maid might abscond with her diamond necklace.*

Word	embezzle, v.
Pronounciation	em-bez-zle
Definition	To steal money or property left in one's care

▶ *The girl's guardian tried to embezzle her inheritance.*

Word	foreclose, v.
Pronounciation	fore-close
Definition	To take and sell a property to pay for a debt

▶ *If you fail to make your mortgage payment, the bank can foreclose on your house.*

Word	forgery, n.
Pronounciation	for-ger-y
Definition	The illegal production of something counterfeit, such as falsifying a document

▶ *When Jim withdrew money from the bank by signing his uncle's name, he was arrested for forgery.*

Exercise 2: Write, Say, Define

Write the Money Misdeeds Vocabulary list in your notebook. Study the pronunciation. Say the words. Write the definitions and indicate whether a word is a noun, a verb, or an adjective.

 Essential

> The word *abscond* comes from the Latin word *abscondere*. The word is a combination of *ab*, away, plus *condere*, store. The words seem to imply taking property (store) and running away with it.

What You've Learned

This section addressed the issue of money-related crimes. It also reminded you how failure to meet financial obligations can result in the loss of your home and other property. If, on the other hand, you happened to be a victim of fraud, such as embezzlement or forgery, the law is on your side. The authorities would try to find and arrest the guilty party and return to you whatever has been stolen.

Wills and Estates

From the legal point of view, a will is a binding document that states how a person wants his property to be distributed after his death. The word *estate* refers to everything that belonged to the deceased. In states that have community property laws, everything that a husband and a wife acquired after marriage is owned jointly. Each spouse owns 50 percent of the total estate. Upon the death of one spouse, the survivor automatically inherits the entire estate. Unmarried couples need wills or at least a written agreement stating how their properties should be divided in case they break up or one of them dies. Without a legal document, a surviving live-in partner cannot claim any part of the shared estate.

Exercise 3: True or False?

Read the following sentences and determine whether they are true or false. Write *T* for true and *F* for false.

Sentences	T or F
A codicil is a handwritten note.	_____
An executor is named in a will.	_____
A holographic will is a copy.	_____
When a person dies intestate, he dies where he was born.	_____

To check your answers, refer to the appendix or the following vocabulary list.

Word	codicil, n.
Pronunciation	cod-i-cil
Definition	A change or explanation added to a will

▶ *A codicil must be written as a formal, legal document.*

Word	executor, n.
Pronunciation	ex-ec-u-tor
Definition	The person named in a will who will comply with the wishes of the decedent

▶ *John was named as the executor of his uncle's will.*

Word	holographic will, n.
Pronunciation	hol-o-graph-ic will
Definition	A handwritten will

▶ *In some states, a holographic will is not valid.*

Word	intestate, adj.
Pronunciation	in-tes-tate
Definition	Dying without a legal will

▶ *When a person dies intestate, there may be a problem settling the estate.*

Alert!

The thirty words that appear in this chapter make up but a small sample of the total number of legal terms that you could expect to find in a law book. The law and the judicial system are so complex and have such a variety of possible interpretations that most legal terms by themselves, without the specific knowledge of an attorney or a judge, can be of little value to the general public. For this reason the simpler more commonly used legal terms were selected.

What You've Learned

In addition to acquainting you with several legal terms that may have not been familiar, the purpose of this section was to stress the importance of making a will. Individuals are advised to review their wills every few years, especially if there have been major changes in their lives. A will is a kindness to your loved ones and an assurance to you that your last wishes will be obeyed. Knowledge of relevant vocabulary will help you carry out this task.

Accidents and Lawsuits

It's a fact of life that accidents happen. An accident has been defined as an event that occurs unexpectedly and is quite unforeseen. Sometimes, however, we behave irresponsibly, taking risks that may lead to an accident. Speeding in heavy traffic, climbing a rickety ladder, and leaving a gate to a fenced swimming pool unlocked are situations that invite trouble. In such cases, a reasonable person should be able to foresee the possibility of serious accidents. When an accident happens and results in an injury, one asks two basic questions. What caused the accident, and who is at fault?

Statistics show that most accidents happen in the home. A woman hurries to answer the telephone, trips over a rug, and breaks her elbow. If she had tripped on that rug before and ignored the danger it presented, then the accident is obviously her fault. A homeowner is replacing a broken front-porch step. He warns a visiting neighbor to be careful as the man prepares to go home. Ignoring the warning, the neighbor falls and breaks his leg. Who's at fault? Since the injured man had been warned, he would probably lose a lawsuit against the homeowner. If an accident occurs due to the carelessness of a landlord, a bus or taxi driver, or the janitorial service in a public building, the injured party could sue for damages and win. In general, the management of any facility that is open to the public can be held responsible for any accident that happens if the mishap occurred as result of proven negligence on their part.

Exercise 4: Definitions: True or False?

Read the words in the left column and decide whether the given definition is true or false. Write *T* for true, *F* for false.

Word	Definition	T or F
arbitrate	To argue	_____
bona fide	A French term	_____
common carrier	A business that transports passengers	_____
damages	Payment for harm or loss	_____
trespass	Complain	_____

To check your answers, refer to the appendix or the following vocabulary list.

Word	arbitrate, v.
Pronunciation	ar-bi-trate
Definition	To settle an argument or quarrel

▶ *A judge may arbitrate a dispute between neighbors.*

Word	bona fide, adj.
Pronunciation	bo-na fide
Definition	A Latin legal term meaning to "speak in good faith"; to speak with good intentions, without deceit

▶ *Ignoring his mother's bona fide warning, Tommy fell when he tried to cross the icy street.*

Word	common carrier, n.
Pronunciation	com-mon car-rier
Definition	A business that charges for transporting passengers, goods, or messages (a bus, taxi, train, etc.)

▶ *When a taxi driver slammed the door on Betty's hand, breaking her fingers, both the driver and the common carrier had to pay for her injuries and suffering.*

Word	damages, n.
Pronunciation	dam-ag-es
Definition	The amount of money that a defendant may be ordered to pay as compensation for any harm or loss

▶ *When sparks from Dan's bonfire set his neighbor's roof on fire, he had to pay for damages to cover the cost of a new roof.*

Word	trespass, v.
Pronunciation	tres-pass
Definition	To enter a building or other property illegally

▶ *Sam warned his son not to trespass; that is, not to walk across their neighbor's field without permission.*

Exercise 5: Write, Say, Define

Write the Accident and Lawsuits words in your notebook. Study the pronunciation. Say the words. Write the definition and indicate whether a word is a noun, a verb, or an adjective.

 Fact

Many legal terms originate from Latin. The word *trespass* comes from the Medieval Latin term *transpassare*. This is a combination of the two words *trans*, which means across, and *passore* which that means a pass such as a mountain pass or border.

Handling Accidents and Lawsuits

If you find yourself in a lawsuit as the result of an accident in which you or another person is injured, or if there is a loss of property, there may be many factors influencing the outcome. Hiring a reputable attorney may be prudent if you cannot settle the matter without a trial.

Victims and Crime

If you've ever been the victim of a crime, you know what a devastating experience that can be. Even a relatively minor crime, such as having your wallet or purse snatched, can have painful repercussions. There may be the loss of a large sum of money or of valuable papers, a credit card, a passport, keys to your home. In addition to these significant losses and the inconvenience of canceling credit cards and replacing a stolen passport, you are left with a feeling of helplessness and violation. A crime that leaves you terrorized and injured can be an unspeakably traumatic experience. Your only recourse is to call or notify the police.

Essential

Most states have a Victims Bill of Rights. These rights guarantee that as a victim you'll be treated with respect, given medical treatment and a safe place to stay, away from your attacker, during a trial. To learn more about your rights as a victim, contact the office of your local prosecuting attorney or your state attorney general.

Informing authorities of a crime committed against you benefits you, as the victim, and society at large. If the criminal is caught, a victim can receive court-ordered compensation for injuries or property loss or damage. By giving the police detailed information about a crime, you can help bring the perpetrator to justice. There is, of course, a hierarchy of crimes ranging from minor mischief to murder. The following Victims and Crime Vocabulary will acquaint you with the most commonly used terms.

Word	assault, n.
Pronunciation	as-sault
Definition	A violent threat or attempt to do bodily harm

▶ *His verbal assault made her run from the room to call the police.*

Word	assault and battery, n.
Pronunciation	as-sault and bat-ter-y
Definition	Violently hitting someone or knocking the person down

▶ *The man was arrested for assault and battery after he hit his wife.*

Word	aggravated assault, n.
Pronunciation	ag-gra-vat-ed as-sault
Definition	A serious physical attack or an attack with a deadly weapon, especially with an intent to commit a crime

▶ *When the robber hit the clerk with his gun, he committed aggravated assault.*

Word	felony, n.
Pronunciation	fel-o-ny
Definition	A serious crime such as murder, rape, or arson

▶ *If you commit a felony, you may be imprisoned for many years.*

Word	misdemeanor, n.
Pronunciation	mis-de-mean-or
Definition	A less serious crime than a felony

▶ *Bob had to pay a fine and serve a short prison term for the misdemeanor of vandalism.*

Exercise 6: Write, Say, Define

Write the Victims and Crime Vocabulary in your notebook. Study the pronunciations. Say the words. Write the definitions and indicate whether a word is a noun, a verb, or an adjective.

What You've Learned

This concludes the section on victims and crime. Awareness that crimes happen and that no one can predict when or how you can become a victim of a criminal act may be your best protection. Even in a "safe" neighborhood, it is prudent to keep your windows and doors locked, especially when you are away from your home and at night. Avoid dark streets and seedy downtown areas. Drive with your car doors locked, and never leave your car with the keys in the ignition. Given the chance, thieves, like birds of prey, can act with lightning speed.

A Day in Court

This final section will acquaint you with a few legal terms that you will hear if you ever have your day in court either as a defendant or a plaintiff. To test your knowledge, refer to Exercise 7.

Exercise 7: Definitions: True or False?

Read the following words and the given definition. Determine if they are true or false. Write *T* for true and *F* for false.

Word	Definition	T or F
arraignment	Judge's robe	_____
commutation	Jurors' discussion	_____
deposition	Sworn testimony	_____

To check your answers, refer to the appendix or the following vocabulary list.

Word	arraignment, n.
Pronunciation	ar-raign-ment
Definition	A court hearing during which the accused answers the charge made against him or her

▶ *During his arraignment, the felon said he was not guilty.*

Word	commutation, n.
Pronunciation	com-mu-ta-tion
Definition	A reduction in a convicted criminal's sentence

▶ *The commutation allowed the pregnant drug dealer to be out of prison before her baby was born.*

Word	deposition, n.
Pronunciation	dep-o-si-tion
Definition	A sworn statement; testimony obtained under oath before a trial

▶ *A woman who saw the car accident gave a deposition.*

Word	expunge, v.
Pronunciation	ex-punge

Definition   To erase completely; to destroy

▶ *After a retrial, the judge was willing to expunge the charge from Bill's criminal record.*

Exercise 8: Write, Say, Define
Write the Court Vocabulary words in your notebook. Study the pronunciation. Say the words. Write the definition and indicate whether a word is a noun, a verb, or an adjective.

Final Review
The following exercises and word play will test your memory and give you a chance to review the legal terms that may have been unfamiliar to you.

Exercise 9: Complete the Words
Read the following, and add the missing letters to complete the terms.

1. a b a n _ _ _ _ _ _ _

2. a d u _ _ _ _ _

3. a l i _ _ _ _

4. b i g _ _ _

5. c u s _ _ _ _

6. s e p _ _ _ _ _ _ _

7. a b s _ _ _ _ _

8. e m b _ _ _ _ _

9. f o r e _ _ _ _ _

10. f o r _ _ _ _

Exercise 10: Add the Missing Word
Read the following two-word terms and add the missing word

1. prenuptial   _____

2. common   _____

3. assault and   _____

4. aggravated   _____

5. holographic   _____

Exercise 11: Find the Vowel
Read the following list of words and fill in the missing vowels: *a, e, i, o, u.*

1. c _ d _ c _ l

2. _ x _ c _ t _ r

3. _ n t _ s t _ t _

4. _ r b _ t r _ t _

5. b _ n _   f _ d _

6. _ x p _ n g _

7. t r _ s p _ s s

8. f _ l _ n y

Exercise 12: Hidden Words Play
Find at least eight hidden words in the following word list.

1. assault
2. annulment
3. misdemeanor
4. arraignment
5. commutation
6. deposition
7. damages

To check your answers to the review exercises, refer to your notebook or earlier parts of this chapter.

Chapter 9
Power Words

Power words are words that evoke an emotional response when they are read or heard. "Give me liberty or give me death" were power words that echoed the determination of a small struggling nation to win independence. "I have a dream" were the inspiring words that fostered the civil rights movement. Today, power words are often used in business arenas, during important meetings, presentations, and negotiations. In this chapter you will be introduced to thirty commonly used executive power words.

Business Meeting Words

People in business have whole lexicons of power words ready to use in times of triumph, crisis, negotiation, or defeat. Several studies have been conducted to discover what business executives identify as essential business power words.

Here's a list of Business Meeting Words:

Word	ascertain, v.
Pronunciation	as-cer-tain
Definition	To determine with certainty

▶ *We must ascertain that these figures are correct.*

Word	augment, v.
Pronunciation	aug-ment
Definition	To enlarge; to increase

▶ *To succeed, we must augment our profits.*

Word	buttress, v.
Pronunciation	but-tress
Definition	To strengthen or support

▶ *You must buttress your argument with data.*

Word	coalesce, v.
Pronunciation	co-a-lesce
Definition	To unite by growth into one unit

▶ *These departments will coalesce into one division under a single manager.*

Exercise 1: Write, Say, Define

Write the Business Meeting Words in your notebook. Study the pronunciation. Say the words. Write the definitions and indicate whether the word is a noun, a verb, or an adjective.

Question?

What group of people often uses power words?
Experienced politicians routinely use power words. Focusing on national and worldwide problems they use fear-evoking words to raise their listeners' level of anxiety. After achieving that goal they resort to comforting promises implying that once they are elected, all will be well. Next time you listen to a political speech, note the power words and how they affect you.

Job Application Words

If you are applying for a position with a large company, it is to your advantage to keep essential power words in mind. As you already know, these are the words executives use and like to hear. These are the words you must know if you want the job. If you are already employed, you could choose these words to negotiate a raise or a promotion, or if you wish to present an idea that would benefit the business as well as your status. Take note of the following Job Application Words and consider how they might be used.

Word	commensurate, adj.
Pronunciation	com-men-su-rate
Definition	Of equal proportion to something else

▶ *Sam named a salary that would be commensurate with his ability.*

Word	competence, n.
Pronunciation	com-pe-tence
Definition	Ability; the state of being able to perform a task

▶ *Jane's resume validated her competence.*

Word	complaisant, adj.
Pronunciation	com-plai-sant
Definition	Agreeable; eager to please

▶ *Ray made it obvious that he would be a complaisant employee.*

Word	expertise, n.
Pronunciation	ex-per-tise
Definition	Specialized knowledge

▶ *Mary's education and experience gave her the expertise that the position required.*

Word	indicative, adj.
Pronunciation	in-dic-a-tive
Definition	Pointing out; showing

▶ *The reference letters were indicative of the young man's ability to do a good job.*

Word	interactive, adj.
Pronunciation	in-ter-ac-tive
Definition	Capable of communicating and working with others

▶ *Walter was hired because he was an interactive person who understood teamwork.*

Exercise 2: Write, Say, Define

Write the Job Application Words in your notebook. Study the pronunciations. Say the words. Write the definitions; indicate whether a word is a noun, a verb, or an adjective.

Alert!

Note the difference between the homophones *complaisant* and *complacent*. Pay attention to the difference in spelling and meaning. A complaisant person is agreeable and cooperative, a complacent person is self-satisfied and may be indifferent to the needs or desires of others.

What You've Learned

As you end this section on Job Application Words, remember that your word list is an example of how power words and the ideas they suggest can help you during a job interview or in the workplace. As you continue through this chapter, you will probably find other equally useful power words.

Business Troubles Vocabulary

Small businesses as well as huge corporations can find themselves in trouble. Many *factors* can affect the success or failure of a company. The state of the national economy can be a major *factor* in whether a business prospers. During a recession, for example, when people are losing their jobs and money is tight, retail businesses, which rely on the purchasing power of their customers, are bound to suffer. Mismanagement, fraud, and power struggles within a corporation can lead to its downfall and financial difficulties. In this section, you will be introduced to power words that are related to business troubles.

 Fact

> Although the word *beleaguered* is now used to describe troublesome situations, such as harassment by creditors, originally the word was a military term. Originating from the Dutch word *belegeren,* it was used to describe a siege, such as when enemy forces surrounded a town of the opposing army, preventing escape.

Word	beleaguered, v.
Pronunciation	be-lea-guered
Definition	To be faced with obstacles; to be overwhelmed by problems

▶ *Facing bankruptcy, the beleaguered CEO suffered a heart attack.*

Word	collusion, n.
Pronunciation	col-lu-sion
Definition	An illegal conspiracy; a secret plot to do harm

▶ *The chairman of the board was accused of collusion with the vice president of the company in an attempt to replace its president.*

Word	gamut, n.
Pronunciation	gam-ut
Definition	A range of something

▶ *Unable to save his failing business, Wilson experienced a gamut of emotions from anger to despair.*

Word	onus, n.
Pronunciation	o-nus
Definition	A burden

▶ *The onus of staggering debt was more than he could bear.*

Word	opprobrium, n.
Pronunciation	op-pro-bri-um
Definition	Disgrace as a result of shameful behavior; reproach

▶ *Her rudeness in dealing with a client brought opprobrium from her supervisor.*

Exercise 3: Write, Say, Define

Write the Business Troubles Words in your notebook. Study the pronunciation. Say the words. Write the definition; indicate whether a word is a noun, a verb, or an adjective.

What You've Learned

Business troubles arise for many reasons. In fact, in many concerns, there are daily crises and troubleshooting is an ongoing strategy. Companies that survive and grow probably have a policy of constant careful monitoring of all aspects of the enterprise. There is a rapport between the top echelon and other staff members and employees. As with other endeavors, a business depends on a harmonious, goal-oriented effort among individuals involved in a mutual undertaking.

Pep Talk Words

An insightful boss, CEO, coach, parent, or teacher knows how to use power words to bolster self-esteem and ambition, to gain approval, and to achieve higher goals. In giving a pep talk, the leader will use terms of praise and recognition of past efforts followed by words that challenge his staff, sports team, or students to achieve even greater success. Study the following words related to pep talks and consider how you could apply such strategies in similar situations.

Word	glean, v.
Pronunciation	gleen
Definition	To gather knowledge or information bit by bit

▶ *A successful businessman will listen to and observe his employees in order to glean a better understanding of their personal and professional needs.*

Word	gumption, n.
Pronunciation	gump-tion
Definition	Shrewd common sense

▶ *The manager advised his team to use gumption when dealing with a difficult client.*

Word	inculcate, v.
Pronunciation	in-cul-cate
Definition	To teach by repetition; to impress an idea by urging or by example

▶ *A good coach will inculcate her players to work and play as a* team.

Word	laud, v.
Pronunciation	laud
Definition	To praise highly

▶ *Mr. Harris was quick to laud a student's improved performance.*

Word	tutelage, n.
Pronunciation	tu-te-lage
Definition	The act of giving close instruction

▶ *Under the supervisor's tutelage, the workers improved their work habits.*

Exercise 4: Write, Say, Define
Write the Pep Talk Words in your notebook. Study the pronunciation. Say the words. Write the definition; indicate whether a word is a noun, a verb, or an adjective.

What You've Learned

It should be clear that the Pep Talk words in your vocabulary are not the actual words that you would use in giving a pep talk. Rather their purpose is to guide you to what can and should be said and how your actions as a boss, coach, parent, or teacher can best build self-esteem and desirable performances among employees, players, children, and students.

 Essential

The word *glean* originates from the Middle French term *gleaner* which means gathering grain or fruit that is left in a field after harvesting. The Gleaners, a famous oil painting by J-F. Millet, depicts three poor peasant women gleaning from the ground the scattered kernels of wheat left after a harvest.

Daily Power Words

At home or at work, speaking with coworkers, friends, and family members, you may use or hear some of the following power words. You may also recognize these words in a book, magazine, or newspaper. Very likely, you'll hear them spoken on TV during a program or a commercial. Listen and notice how many of the power words are now familiar to you.

Here's a list of Daily Power Words:

Word	cohort, n.
Pronunciation	co-hort
Definition	An associate or companion with shared interests

▶ *Meg and her cohort Sally opened their own veterinarian clinic.*

Word	commiserate, v.
Pronunciation	com-mis-er-ate
Definition	To share someone's misfortune or sadness

▶ *Frank was the first to commiserate with Joe when the boy's bike was stolen.*

Word	innate, adj.
Pronunciation	in-nate
Definition	Inborn; possessed as part of a person's personality

▶ *Her innate sense of integrity earned her a promotion.*

Word	nebulous, adj.
Pronunciation	neb-u-lous
Definition	Vague, hazy

▶ *The speaker's nebulous remarks were difficult to understand.*

Word	nepotism, n.
Pronunciation	nep-o-tism
Definition	Favoritism toward a relative in a business situation

▶ *Everyone resented their boss's nepotism when he promoted a nephew in place of a better qualified employee.*

Word	ostensibly, adv.
Pronunciation	os-ten-si-bly
Definition	Seeming or appearing to be true

▶ *He was ostensibly going on a business trip when in fact he went to visit a girlfriend.*

Exercise 5: Write, Say, Define
Write the Daily Power Words in your notebook. Study the pronunciation. Say the words. Write the definition; indicate whether a word is a noun, a verb, or an adjective.

What You've Learned
The conclusion of this section brings you twenty-five power words that are commonly used by executives in the business world. Your next section will address the vital topic of business and personal negotiations. Words relating to the subject will be part of your power words vocabulary.

Negotiation
Negotiations occur to settle disputes and make business deals. Everyone negotiates with someone many times a day. Children negotiate with their parents for a later bedtime, a bigger allowance, or a special treat. Two women would like to meet for lunch. Both are employed and both have family-related responsibilities and very little free time. The ladies begin negotiating regarding a time and day that they can get together. Business or financial negotiations between corporations are far more serious.

Each side has its own goals and expectations, and neither is willing to lose out on a deal. An agreement is reached when the two sides reach a compromise and make concessions for an equitable settlement. New words to add to your vocabulary list will focus on negotiating skills.

Word	assertive, adj.
Pronunciation	as-ser-tive
Definition	Inclined to self-confidence and boldness in expressing an opinion

▶ *An experienced negotiator is assertive but calm and polite.*

Word	belligerent, adj.
Pronunciation	bel-lig-er-ent
Definition	Displaying angry, combative behavior

▶ *A belligerent attitude indicates a weakness in a negotiator's position.*

Word	concession, n.
Pronunciation	con-ces-sion
Definition	The act of yielding or giving in on some point in a negotiation

▶ *A skilled negotiator knows when it is to her advantage to make a concession.*

Word	consummate, v.
Pronunciation	con-sum-mate
Definition	To finalize; to close a deal

▶ *The goal of every negotiation is to reach an agreement and to consummate a settlement.*

Word	reciprocity, n.
Pronunciation	rec-i-proc-i-ty
Definition	The act of exchanging favors; trading for a mutual benefit

▶ *Reciprocity plays a major role in the process of negotiation.*

Exercise 6: Write, Say, Define

Write the Negotiation Words in your notebook. Study the pronunciation. Say the words. Write the definition; indicate whether a word is a noun, a verb, or an adjective.

 Fact

> Like many other English words that come from Latin, *cohort* is the Latin for one of the ten divisions of a Roman legion. A legion was the principal unit of the Roman army, consisting of three to six thousand foot soldiers and a cavalry. *Cohort* refers to a military division in which the men form particularly close comradeship.

What You've Learned

This brings the section on negotiation to a close. The process of negotiation is a complex and fascinating activity. Like a chess game, it involves strategic moves and specific rules that successful players follow religiously. One rule that was mentioned in your word list is the rule of reciprocity. Reciprocity implies something that children call tit-for-tat. As you go about your daily business, such exchanges between you and a friend, or your spouse may come to mind. "If you get the data, I'll make the graphs," you might suggest to a colleague as you prepare for a conference. "If you take the kids to soccer practice tomorrow, I'll do it next week." When a couple exchanges rings in a wedding ceremony that is a symbolic act of reciprocity. Remember the importance of reciprocity next time you are negotiating an important issue.

Final Review
Now it's time for a final review of what you've learned in this chapter.

Exercise 7: Find the Vowel
Read the following incomplete words and fill in the missing vowels; *a, e, i, o, u.*

1. _ s c _ r t _ _ n

2. _ _ g m _ n t

3. b _ t t r _ s s

4. c _ _ l _ s c _

5. c _ m m _ n s _ r _ t _

6. c _ m p _ t _ n c _

7. c _ m p l _ _ s _ n t

8. _ x p _ r t _ s _

9. _ n d _ c t _ v _

10. _ n t _ r _ c t _ v _

Exercise 8: Complete the Words
Read the first few letters and complete the following words.

1. b e l _ _ _ _ _ _ _ _

2. c o l l u _ _ _ _

3. g a _ _ _

4. o n _ _

5. o p p r o _ _ _ _ _

6. g u m _ _ _ _ _

7. g l e _ _

8. i n c u _ _ _ _ _

9. l a _ _

10. t u t _ _ _ _ _

Exercise 9: Word Definitions
Read the given definitions and write the correct vocabulary words.

Definition	Word
angry	b _ _ _ _ _ _ _ _ _ _
fair exchange	r _ _ _ _ _ _ _ _ _ _
self-confident	a _ _ _ _ _ _ _
finalize	c _ _ _ _ _ _ _ _
yielding	c _ _ _ _ _ _ _ _ _

Exercise 10: Definitions: True or False?
Read the vocabulary words and the given definitions. Write *T* for true, *F* for false.

Word	Definition	T or F
nepotism	Hatred	_____
commiserate	Ignore	_____
innate	Inborn trait	_____
cohort	A joke	_____
nebulous	Vague	_____

To check your answers, refer to the appendix.

In this chapter you were given a sampling of power words and how these words might be used in six different situations. As you may recall, these situations were a business conference, a job application, business troubles, pep talks, the daily use of power words in negotiating a deal. You should remember that power words have the ability to evoke an emotional response in the reader or listener. As a speaker, for example, you should decide ahead of time how you want your words to affect your audience. Do you wish to arouse fear or anger, or do you wish to encourage, inspire, or reassure your listeners? It all depends on what you wish to accomplish.

Chapter 10
Action and Event Words

There is an interesting relationship between the two nouns *action* and *event*. The word *action* comes from the verb *to act*. It implies something that is done, as well as some kind of movement or behavior. An event cannot occur without a preceding action. An event is a happening, the consequence of an action. For example, the event of a birthday party depends on the actions of the hostess who makes all the necessary arrangements for the celebration.

Positive Action Words

People do many things. Actions fill our lives twenty-four hours a day. Some of our actions like breathing and sleeping are automatic; they are the mechanisms of our body. Aside from the hours when we sleep, our days are a continuum of routine activities (actions). We know what they are. The list is long, involving work, interactions with people, the essential chores of caring for a home and family, shopping, cooking, and the personal needs of dressing, grooming, eating, and relaxing.

 Fact

The word *philanthropy* originates both from late Latin and Greek. The Greek word *phileean*, which means love plus the word *anthropos*, meaning man, gives us the English term *philanthropy*, love of mankind. Philadelphia, which has been called the "City of Brotherly Love," probably got its name from the Greek word *phileean*.

Within the rather mundane routine of daily behavior, there are instances of goodness and kindness. Your Positive Action Words will give you a descriptive sample of such deeds.

Word	benevolence, n.
Pronunciation	be-nev-o-lence
Definition	A desire to do kindness

▶ *Little Mary took to heart the story of the Good Samaritan's benevolence.*

Word	charitable, adj.
Pronunciation	char-i-ta-ble
Definition	Generous in giving gifts and help to the poor

▶ *Thomas was a charitable man who used his wealth to help the poor peasants in his village.*

Word	magnanimity, n.
Pronunciation	mag-na-nim-i-ty
Definition	Generosity of mind, forgiving

▶ *Anne's magnanimity enabled her to forgive her uncle's thoughtlessness in her time of need.*

Word	philanthropy, n.
Pronunciation	phi-lan-thro-py
Definition	The love of humankind, shown through practical actions, gifts of money, and support of worthy causes

▶ *Her love of knowledge and philanthropy paid for the education of many deserving students.*

Word	solicitous, adj.
Pronunciation	so-lic-i-tous
Definition	Concerned or anxious about something or someone

▶ *Solicitous about the welfare of her old aunt, Kelly took time to visit her every day.*

Exercise 1: Write, Say, Define

Write the Positive Action Words in your notebook. Study the pronunciations. Say the words. Write the definitions and indicate whether a word is a noun, a verb, or an adjective.

What You've Learned

This concludes the first section of this chapter on actions and events. As you study your new vocabulary words, you may think of your positive actions as well as those of people who have been kind to you or whose generous actions brought media recognition. In the next section, we will address less desirable actions.

Negative Action Words

Unfortunately, negative behaviors are more likely to get attention than positive actions. The bad deeds of villains in books and movies are often more entertaining than good behaviors. It may be because villainous actions create more drama and arouse sharper emotions of fear, indignation, and combativeness. Little boys dream of being the hero who gets the "bad" guy. In a sense, good triumphs over evil and positive actions are rewarded. Nevertheless, the next set of words will introduce you to negative actions.

Word	iniquitous, adj.
Pronunciation	in-iq-ui-tous
Definition	Characterized by wickedness

▶ *It was iniquitous of Joan to spread false rumors about her rival at work.*

Word	malicious, adj.
Pronunciation	ma-li-cious
Definition	Resulting from hatred, ill-will, or a desire to harm

▶ *Spray-painting her ex-husband's SUV was a malicious thing to do.*

Word	ruthless, adj.
Pronunciation	ruth-less
Definition	Merciless; cruel; having no compassion

▶ *The ruthless cruelty of the invading barbarians terrified the population.*

Word	transgression, n.
Pronunciation	trans-gres-sion
Definition	A violation of a rule; a sin

▶ *Max was tempted to cheat on the exam but he knew it would be a major transgression.*

Word	vindictive, adj.
Pronunciation	vin-dic-tive
Definition	Mean-spirited; eager for revenge

▶ *In a vindictive fit, Lynn destroyed her sister's homework.*

Exercise 2: Write, Say, Define

Write the Negative Action Words in your notebook. Study the pronunciation. Say the words. Write the definitions and indicate whether a word is a noun, verb, or adjective.

 Essential

> The word *transgression* is derived from the Latin word *transgressus*, which in turn is composed of two words, *trans,* which means across, and *gradi,* which means step. Combined, the words could be understood to imply crossing or stepping over a boundary. In English, as you know, it means breaking a rule or law.

Naughty Action Words

The term naughty can have two connotations depending on how the word is interpreted. To some people, it signifies unruly, disobedient, even wicked behavior. Other people may interpret the word in a more lighthearted way. They think of naughty as something that describes innocent, funny trickery and pranks. The Naughty Action Words will focus on the lighthearted interpretation of the word *naughty*.

Words	frivolity, n.
Pronunciation	fri-vol-i-ty
Definition	Foolish, lighthearted, noisy, silly behavior.

▶ *A neighbor called the police when the young people's frivolity on the beach became too noisy.*

Words	impish, adj.
Pronunciation	imp-ish
Definition	Exhibiting playful, teasing, or joking behavior

▶ *Kevin had an impish grin on his face when he drew a funny birthday card for his dad.*

Words	mischievous, adj.
Pronunciation	mis-chie-vous
Definition	Playful in a teasing way

▶ *The mischievous twins Mindy and Lindy planned many April Fool's jokes.*

Words	prankishness, n.
Pronunciation	prank-ish-ness
Definition	The act of playing pranks or tricks on people.

▶ *Eddie made people laugh, but eventually his prankishness began to annoy his roommate.*

Exercise 3: Write, Say, Define

Write the Naughty Action Words in your notebook. Study the pronunciation. Say the words. Write the definitions and indicate whether a word is a noun, a verb, or an adjective.

Fact

In 1935 there was an Oscar-winning film, a musical titled *Naughty Marietta*. The title roles were acted and sung by Jeanette MacDonald and Eddy Nelson. This was a fun, entertaining movie about a princess who escapes from an arranged marriage by disguising herself as a maid and sailing for New Orleans. She is captured by pirates and saved by the hero and all ends well. This is an example of lighthearted naughtiness.

Happy Events

In this section, the words will refer to grand, festive events that are specially arranged to celebrate or commemorate a memorable milestone in someone's life. These are events that occur because someone took the initiative to make them happen. They are the result of an action. Refer to Exercise 4 to test your knowledge of the Happy Events Vocabulary.

Exercise 4: Definitions: True or False?

Read the following words. Determine whether the definitions are true or false. Write *T* for true, *F* for false.

Word	Definition	T or F
bacchanal	Card game	_____
centennial	A hundredth anniversary	_____
commemoration	Celebration in remembrance	_____

jubilee	A dessert	_____
matriculation	Admission to college	_____
nuptials	Small rodents	_____

To check your answers, refer to the appendix or the following vocabulary list.

Word	bacchanal, n.
Pronunciation	bac-cha-nal
Definition	A drunken orgy

▶ *Worshipers of Bacchus would attend a bacchanal.*

Word	centennial, n.
Pronunciation	cen-ten-ni-al
Definition	A hundredth anniversary

▶ *The small town celebrated its centennial with a parade, dancing in the streets, and fireworks.*

Word	commemoration, n.
Pronunciation	com-mem-o-ra-tion
Definition	A celebration in memory of a person or of an outstanding event

▶ *In John's family, the commemoration of Independence Day was a big celebration.*

Word	jubilee, n.
Pronunciation	ju-bi-lee
Definition	Any season of rejoicing and festivity

▶ *The king celebrated the fifteenth year of his monarchy with a nationwide jubilee.*

Word	matriculation, n.
Pronunciation	ma-tric-u-la-tion
Definition	Admission into college

▶ *Joe's entire family was proud of his matriculation to the university.*

Word	nuptials, n.
Pronunciation	nup-tials
Definition	Of or relating to a wedding

▶ *Their nuptials were a solemn ceremony.*

 Essential

In addition to describing the celebration of special anniversaries and other occasions, the word *jubilee* has a historical and religious connotation. In Jewish history, jubilee occurred on every fiftieth year from the entrance of the Hebrews into Canaan. In the Roman Catholic Church, Jubilee is a year of special indulgence as proclaimed by the Pope.

Exercise 5: Write, Say, Define

Write the Happy Events Vocabulary in your notebook. Study the pronunciation. Say the words. Write the definitions and indicate whether a word is a noun, a verb, or an adjective.

Sad Events

Of course, there is more to life than just graduations, weddings, and jubilees. There are also times of sadness and mourning. We also have words to express and describe these emotions. In most cases, illness, death, and other misfortunes are events over which we have no control. It is true, however, that sometimes something bad—a car accident, for example—can happen as a result of another person's negligent actions. In any circumstances, knowing how to talk about a sad event can bring comfort.

Here is a list of Sad Events Vocabulary:

Word	disconsolate, adj.
Pronunciation	dis-con-so-late
Definition	Unable to overcome sadness

▶ *After Albert died, the disconsolate Queen Victoria wore black for the rest of her life.*

Word	doleful, adj.
Pronunciation	dole-ful
Definition	Sad; depressed

▶ *When Ron lost his job, he became doleful and withdrawn.*

Word	funereal, adj.
Pronunciation	fu-ne-re-al
Definition	Of or related to a funeral; dark; gloomy; mournful

▶ *Two black horses with black plumes on their heads lead the funereal procession.*

Word	grievous, adj.
Pronunciation	grie-vous
Definition	Causing grief, distress, or severe injury

▶ *When Mark fell off the cliff, he suffered grievous injuries.*

Word	lamentation, n.
Pronunciation	lam-en-ta-tion
Definition	An expression of mourning or sorrow

▶ *Julie's lamentation over her broken love affair troubled her friends.*

 Question?

What is the origin of the word *doleful*?

Doleful is derived from the English word *dole*, which refers to government relief paid to the unemployed from a special fund contributed by workers. The origin of *dole* is the late Latin term *dolium*, which means grief. Very likely the Spanish word for pain, *dolor*, also originates from Latin.

Exercise 6: Write, Say, Define

Write the Sad Events Vocabulary in your notebook. Study the pronunciation. Say the words. Write the definitions and indicate whether a word is a noun, a verb, or an adjective.

Disastrous Events

Now we turn our attention to events caused by natural phenomena, which are in most instances unexpected and beyond our control. Throughout history, horrendous natural disasters have occurred all over the world bringing death and suffering to millions of people. Earthquakes, floods, volcanic eruptions, tornadoes, and hurricanes have shown their deadly power. Once again, humans have developed a vocabulary for naming and describing these devastating events.

Word	calamity, n.
Pronunciation	ca-lam-i-ty
Definition	A destructive event that brings terrible loss

▶ *The influenza epidemic was a worldwide calamity.*

Word	catastrophe, n.
Pronunciation	ca-tas-tro-phe
Definition	An enormous, destructive occurrence; a complete failure

▶ *The tsunami that hit Indonesia and the coasts of other Asian countries was a catastrophe that will never be forgotten.*

Word	conflagration, n.
Pronunciation	con-fla-gra-tion
Definition	An inferno; a huge fire

▶ *The wildfire was a conflagration that burned thousands of acres.*

Word	deluge, n.
Pronunciation	del-uge
Definition	A great flood

▶ *The biblical flood that Noah survived was a deluge.*

Word	tempest, n.
Pronunciation	tem-pest
Definition	A violent windstorm often accompanied by rain, hail, or snow

▶ *A tempest left them shipwrecked on an uninhabited island.*

 Fact

> *The Deluge* is a dramatic interpretation of the biblical flood by the well-known engraver of biblical stories, Gustav Doré. The word *deluge* comes from the Middle French term *deluvere*, originating from the Latin word *diluvium* and meaning to wash away.

Exercise 7: Write, Say, Define

Write the Disastrous Events Vocabulary in your notebook. Study the pronunciation. Say the words. Write the definitions and indicate whether a word is a noun, a verb, or an adjective.

Final Review

You now have the opportunity of reviewing the Action and Event Words presented in this chapter. The following exercises and word play should refresh your memory.

Exercise 8: Complete the Words

Read the beginning of the following words and add the missing final letters.

1. b e n e _ _ _ _ _ _ _
2. c h a r _ _ _ _ _ _
3. s o l i _ _ _ _ _ _
4. p h i l a _ _ _ _ _ _ _
5. m a g n a _ _ _ _ _ _
6. i n i q u _ _ _ _ _
7. m a l _ _ _ _ _ _ _
8. r u t h _ _ _ _
9. t r a n s _ _ _ _ _ _ _ _ _
10. v i n _ _ _ _ _ _ _

Exercise 9: Hidden Words Play
Read the following words and find at least four to ten hidden words in the parent words.

1. impish
2. prankishness
3. mischievous
4. frivolity
5. doleful
6. funereal
7. lamentation

Exercise 10: Add the Missing Consonant
Read the following and add the missing consonants.

1. g _ i e _ o u _
2. d i _ _ o _ s o _ a _ e
3. n u _ _ i a _ _
4. m a t _ _ c u l a _ i o _
5. b a c _ _ a _ a _
6. c e _ t e _ _ i a _
7. c o m _ e _ o _ a _ i o _

Exercise 11: Add the Vowels

Read the following and add the missing vowels.

1. c _ l _ m _ t y

2. c _ t _ s t r _ p h e

3. c _ n f l _ g r _ t _ _ n

4. d _ l _ g _

5. t _ m p _ s t

6. j _ b _ l _ _

To check your answers, refer to the appendix.

This chapter gave you words that are related to actions and events that are positive, negative, and at times disastrous. Our own actions and how we react to events, whether good or bad, govern our lives. Our actions reveal to the world the desirable and undesirable aspects of our personalities. Inevitably, misfortunes and sad events will occur. It is also possible that you may wish to make a change. Consider then what you can do, and what actions you can undertake to realize your goal or ease the pain of a sad event.

Chapter 11
Appearance and Character Words

When you're describing a person to a friend or coworker, depending upon whether you like or dislike the individual, you probably limit your vocabulary to a few words such as, "He's good looking and nice," or if you dislike the man or woman you might say, "He's a jerk," or "She's a busybody, a real pain in the neck." If these examples sound familiar, it may be time to expand your vocabulary, using words that can describe a person in a much more colorful and articulate manner.

Negative First Impressions

When a strange man or woman appears at your door or place of business, you will usually get a quick mental impression of the person's appearance. Along with that mental picture, you experience an inner reaction of either approval or disapproval. "Clothes make the man," an old saying reminds us. This is still true. To make a good first impression, make an effort to dress with care. There's no denying the fact that styles and dress etiquette have undergone great changes. Clothes today are far more casual. Nevertheless, there is a marked difference in how we react to someone wearing clean, well-fitting jeans and an attractive top or shirt to someone wearing a pair of baggy, ragged pants and a filthy undershirt.

The following words describe the appearance and clothes that are likely to give a negative first impression.

Word	disheveled, adj.
Pronunciation	di-shev-eled
Definition	Untidy, rumpled

▶ *The old woman's disheveled appearance embarrassed her family.*

Word	sloppiness, n.
Pronunciation	slop-pi-ness
Definition	Untidiness

▶ *Their son's sloppiness angered his parents.*

Word	slovenly, adj.
Pronunciation	slov-en-ly
Definition	Dressed neglectfully, carelessly

▶ *The young waitress was repulsed by the man's slovenly attire.*

Word	tawdry, adj.
Pronunciation	taw-dry
Definition	Gaudy and cheap in appearance

▶ *Against her mother's advice, Toni wore a tawdry dress to the prom.*

Word	unkempt, adj.
Pronunciation	un-kempt
Definition	Uncombed; messy

▶ *The man's unkempt long hair and beard frightened the bank teller.*

 **Question?**

What is the origin of the word *disheveled*?
The word *disheveled* comes from Old French and consists of two words, *des*, meaning apart, and *chevel*, meaning hair. When the two words are combined, *des* plus *chevel* form *deschevel*, which implies disarranged hair or dress. Originating from French, the English word *disheveled* also refers to ungroomed hair and rumpled clothing.

Exercise 1: Write, Say, Define
Write the Negative First Impression Words in your notebook. Study the pronunciation. Say the words. Write the definition and indicate whether a word is a noun, a verb, or an adjective.

Negative Physical Appearances

It is human nature to be repelled by something that we find extremely unattractive or frightening. While you don't want to use words such as those that follow to offend people, such words may come into your life in other ways. For example, writers often use words denoting negative physical appearance to describe villainous or evil characters. Knowledge of such words will help you in both your reading endeavors and, if you personally try your hand at writing, your own creative works.

 Fact

> Gargoyles were waterspouts built on public buildings during the Middle Ages. They were carved to represent hideous human and animal figures. The use of gargoyles as waterspouts, was started by ancient Greek architects, but it was during the Middle Ages that gargoyles became a decorative architectural addition.

Word	corpulent, adj.
Pronunciation	cor-pu-lent
Definition	Obese; overweight

▶ *The corpulent man could no longer fasten his coat.*

Word	harridan, n.
Pronunciation	har-ri-dan
Definition	A scolding, vicious woman

▶ *Joan's mother-in-law was a harridan who made Joan's life miserable.*

Word	repugnant, adj.
Pronunciation	re-pug-nant
Definition	Arousing strong feelings of dislike

▶ *Her landlord's scowling face was so repugnant to Amy, she decided to find another apartment.*

Word	ungainly, adj.
Pronunciation	un-gain-ly
Definition	Awkward; clumsy

▶ *The tall, thin boy was ungainly, but everyone liked his cheerful smile.*

Exercise 2: Write, Say, Define

Write the Negative Physical Appearance Words in your notebook. Study the pronunciation. Say the words. Write the definition and indicate whether a word is a noun, a verb, or an adjective.

Negative Personality Traits

Just as we may be unjustly repulsed by a malformed body or face, we can be just as easily blindly attracted by a handsome face and a well-built physique of a man or the alluring smile and curves of a woman. In each instance, we can be deceived. Outward beauty may hide ugly character flaws, and the reverse is equally true.

Exercise 3: Test Your Knowledge

Read the following Negative Personality Traits Vocabulary, and select the correct antonym from the following list: *truthful, sweet, friendly, pure, sincere.*

Word	Antonym
acrimonious	_____
mendacious	_____
pugnacious	_____
salacious	_____
sycophant	_____

To check your answers, refer to the appendix or the following vocabulary list.

Word	acrimonious, adj.
Pronunciation	ac-ri-mo-ni-ous
Definition	Bitter; ill-natured

▶ *His acrimonious attitude alienated his employees.*

Word	mendacious, adj.
Pronunciation	men-da-cious
Definition	Lying; untruthful

▶ *Sue's mendacious gossip left her friendless.*

Word	pugnacious, adj.
Pronunciation	pug-na-cious
Definition	Quarrelsome; combative

▶ *Tom's pugnacious nature landed him in jail.*

Word	salacious, adj.
Pronunciation	sa-la-cious
Definition	Lewd; dirty-minded

▶ *Offended by her date's salacious remarks, Sally left the restaurant.*

Word	sycophant, n.
Pronunciation	syc-o-phant
Definition	An ambitious, insincere flatterer

▶ *A skilled sycophant, Jones wooed and married a wealthy old widow.*

Alert!

The word *sycophant* originates from the Latin word *sycophanta* and Greek word *sycophantes*. In both languages *sycophant* means informer or swindler. In English, as you already know, the term describes a self-serving insincere flatterer. If anyone ever calls you a sycophant, you may want to examine your behavior!

Exercise 4: Write, Say, Define

Write the Negative Personality Traits Vocabulary in your notebook. Study the pronunciation. Say the words. Write the definition and indicate whether a word is a noun, a verb, or an adjective.

Positive First Impressions

Although it's fashionable for well-dressed individuals to wear chic casual clothes, numerous professions require an almost uniform style of attire among their top-ranking employees. Law firms, Wall Street, the media, and other major corporations set the tone on how their associates should dress. The image that comes to mind for men and women is the "power suit." Almost without deviation, men wear dark suits, white shirts, and conservative silk ties. Women wear jackets and shirts or pantsuits. Although women are allowed a wider range of colors and styles of blouse, the total effect remains conservative and fashionably discreet. If you enter a cosmopolitan establishment wearing a "power suit," you will present a favorable first impression.

Here's a list of some Positive First Impression vocabulary:

Word	believability, adj.
Pronunciation	be-liev-a-bil-i-ty
Definition	Capable of evoking trust

▶ *Spike heels or a frilly blouse would spoil the believability of her "power suit" attire.*

Word	elegant, adj.
Pronunciation	el-e-gant
Definition	Tasteful; fine in dress, manners, and general appearance

▶ *Her expensive black gown was elegant in its simplicity.*

Word	fastidious, adj.
Pronunciation	fas-tid-i-ous
Definition	Being careful about detail

▶ *Nancy was so fastidious about her hair, her makeup, and her clothes that it took her an hour to get dressed.*

Word	immaculate, adj.
Pronunciation	im-mac-u-late
Definition	Spotless; perfectly clean

▶ *She wore immaculate white gloves to the ceremony.*

Word	impeccable, adj.
Pronunciation	im-pec-ca-ble
Definition	Flawless; virtually perfect

▶ *Ken, a man of impeccable taste in clothing, served as an example to his colleagues.*

Exercise 5: Write, Say, Define

Write the Positive First Impression Words in your notebook. Study the pronunciation. Say the words. Write the definition and indicate whether a word is a noun, a verb, or an adjective.

Fact

George "Beau" Brummel (1778–1840) was considered a dandy for his conspicuous elegance; nevertheless his style of dress influenced English society and spread throughout Europe. He was also known as a wit and an authority on fashions. The words *Beau Brummel* are now used to describe a dandy.

Positive Physical Appearance

Beauty, it is said, is in the eyes of the beholder. The statement is undoubtedly true. We all have our preferences and our ways of describing a person we consider to be attractive. We refer to them as beautiful, gorgeous, glamorous, manly, handsome, sexy, or, as young girls say, a "hunk." Romance novelists describe their heroes and heroines in many ways, depicting their eyes, their hair, and their bodies. Men are usually tall and muscular with broad shoulders and slim hips. The women have slender curvaceous figures and are either tall or petite.

Popular magazines frequently feature photographs of the ten best-looking bachelors or the ten most beautiful young women in Hollywood. History and mythology have their own lists of famous beauties and heroic, handsome men. Helen of Troy, Cleopatra, and Aphrodite, the Greek goddess of love and sex, top the list of women.

Michelangelo Buonarroti's famous sculpture of the biblical David is an example of masculine handsomeness. The vocabulary list in this section will offer words that describe physical attractiveness.

 Essential

> The adjective *winsome* is derived from the Old English word *wynsum*. *Wynsum* comes from the word *wynn*, which means joy. The word *lithesome* originates from the Old English term *lithe*, which means gentle.

Word	Adonis, n.
Pronunciation	A-don-is
Definition	A Greek god, a symbol of masculine physical perfection

▶ *Lucy called the good-looking lifeguard her Adonis.*

Word	enchanting, adj.
Pronunciation	en-chant-ing
Definition	Delightful; charming; alluring

▶ *Ivy greeted him with an enchanting smile.*

Word	lithesome, adj.
Pronunciation	lithe-some
Definition	Graceful; supple; pliant

▶ *The ballerina's lithesome movements charmed her audience.*

Word	pulchritude, n.
Pronunciation	pul-chri-tude
Definition	Beauty; a beautiful figure

▶ *The marble statue captured the goddess's feminine pulchritude.*

Word	winsome, adj.
Pronunciation	win-some
Definition	Charming, in a childlike way; cheerful; attractive

▶ *The barmaid's winsome appearance attracted the male customers.*

Exercise 6: Write, Say, Define

Write the Positive Physical Appearance Words in your notebook. Study the pronunciation. Say the words. Write the definition and indicate whether a word is a noun, a verb, or an adjective.

Positive Personality Traits

A pleasant personality is a valuable asset. In the long run it has greater power than sheer physical beauty in attracting friends and in maintaining loving relationships. Few of us are blessed with the perfection of an ideally beautiful figure or face. Without a major makeover, we have no choice but to accept our bodies and features. Our personality traits, however, are more malleable. We can recognize and correct flaws in attitudes, relationships, or behavior. With time, beauty can fade, but a positive personality is ageless.

Word	charisma, n.
Pronunciation	cha-ris-ma
Definition	A quality of leadership, confidence, and personal appeal

▶ *The teacher's charisma inspired her pupils.*

Word	debonair, adj.
Pronunciation	deb-o-nair
Definition	Suave; polite; charming

▶ *Paul's debonair manner ensured his acceptance into high society.*

Word	solicitous, adj.
Pronunciation	so-lic-i-tous
Definition	Anxious or concerned; eager to help; attentive to the needs of others

▶ *A solicitous nurse was very kind to me during my illness.*

Word	staunchness, n.
Pronunciation	staunch-ness
Definition	Loyalty

▶ *Janet endured her husband's financial reverses with admirable staunchness.*

Word	virtuous, adj.
Pronunciation	vir-tu-ous
Definition	Having high moral principles; honest

▶ *I can trust Alice, a virtuous woman.*

Exercise 7: Write, Say, Define

Write the Positive Personality Traits Vocabulary in your notebook. Study the pronunciation. Say the words. Write the definition and indicate whether a word is a noun, a verb, or an adjective.

Final Review

You've nearly reached the end of Chapter 11, so now it's time to see what you've learned. The following exercises and word play will give you a chance to test yourself on how well you have assimilated formerly unfamiliar words.

Exercise 8: Complete the Words

Read the following list; add the missing letters to complete the words.

1. dish _ _ _ _ _ _

2. unk _ _ _ _

3. slov _ _ _ _

4. taw _ _ _

5. slop _ _ _ _ _ _

6. corp _ _ _ _ _

7. har _ _ _ _ _

8. repu _ _ _ _ _

9. unga _ _ _ _

Exercise 9: Find the Consonant

Read the following list and fill in the missing consonants.

1. a c _ i _ o n i o u _

2. m e _ _ a c i o u _

3. s y _ o _ h a _ _

4. s a _ a _ i o u _

5. p u _ _ a _ i o u _

6. b e _ i e _ a _ i _ i _ y

Exercise 10: Find the Vowels

Read the following list and fill in the missing vowels.

1. _ l _ g _ n t

2. f _ s t _ d _ _ _ s

3. _ m m _ c _ l _ t _

4. _ m p _ c c _ b l _

5. _ d _ n _ s

6. _ n c h _ n t _ n g

Exercise 11: Supply the Right Word

Read the following definitions and write the word that fits the definition.

Graceful; pliant _____

Physical beauty _____

A quality of leadership; appeal _____

Suave; charming; attractive _____

Exercise 12: Hidden Words

Read the following words and find six to ten hidden words from each of the parent words.

To check your answers, refer to the appendix.

1. believability
2. charisma
3. debonair
4. solicitous
5. staunchness
6. virtuous

Chapter 12
Fine Arts Vocabulary

The arts is a general term that is applied to human creative endeavors. The word *art* can be used to describe just about anything that we make as long as it is done well and with obvious talent or skill. There are also industrial, scientific, and horticultural arts, as well as many other categories that illustrate human achievement. This chapter will focus on fine arts, a term used to designate aesthetic works in the fields of music, painting, drawing, sculpture, dance, and literature.

A Night at the Opera

Opera is a story, a play in which music is the dominant factor. Against an orchestral background, all dialogue is sung, rather than spoken. The scenery is usually very elaborate. As the drama or the story unfolds, you can expect to hear solos, duets, and choruses. Very often, there are scenes with dancing in glamorous ballrooms or even in the street. Although there are lighthearted, humorous operas, the grand operas have a serious theme, a complex plot with a tragic ending. If you go to a grand opera in a metropolitan city, you can expect to hear and see world-famous performers with mesmerizing voices and beautiful music played by excellent musicians.

Here is a list of opera vocabulary.

Word	aria, n.
Pronunciation	a-ri-a
Definition	A song for a single voice, usually the highlight of a scene, designed to express the inner emotions of the character, either sad or joyous (Arias can be very dramatic and difficult to sing, challenging the singer's voice and skill.)

▶ *The beautiful, heart-rending aria brought tears to Carol's eyes.*

Word	basso profundo, n.
Pronunciation	bas-so pro-fun-do
Definition	A deep bass singing voice

▶ *Paul Robeson and Feodor Chalapin were famous for their basso profundos.*

Word	coloratura, n.
Pronunciation	col-or-a-tu-ra
Definition	A soprano singer who specializes in high, light, flexible passages

▶ *The coloratura's clean, high notes, trills, and runs thrilled her audience.*

Word	libretto, n.
Pronunciation	li-bret-to
Definition	A book containing the words of an opera

▶ *The libretto for the opera* Faust *was based on a medieval legend.*

Word	overture, n.
Pronunciation	o-ver-ture
Definition	An orchestral prelude, or introduction, to an opera that sets the tone and mood for the dramatic performances

▶ *The somber overture sent shivers down Dora's spine.*

Exercise 1: Write, Say, Define
Write the Opera Vocabulary in your notebook. Study the pronunciation. Say the words. Write the definitions and indicate whether a word is a noun, a verb, or an adjective.

A Symphony Concert
Basically, the word *symphony* means "a harmonious or agreeable mingling of sound." It can also mean an agreeable blending of other things, such as colors in a painting.

Musically speaking, a symphony is a long complex composition, written for an orchestra.

A symphonic orchestra usually consists of string, brass, woodwind, and percussion sections. Violins, violas, cellos, and a harp are in the string section. Horns and trumpets are in the brass section. Flutes, oboes, clarinets, and bassoons compose the woodwind section. A kettledrum, cymbals, bells, clappers, and other noise-producing instruments make up the percussion section.

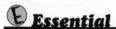 **Essential**

> A sonata is a musical composition for one or two instruments that follows the format of a symphony. Akin to the symphony a sonata has three or four movements. Again each movement is different in tempo and mood, but in the end the movements come together in a cohesive whole. Beethoven wrote sonatas for the piano, violin, and cello. His best known piano sonatas are the *Emperor,* the *Moonlight,* and the *Pathetique.*

A symphony usually has four movements. The first sets the tone and theme of the entire work. The second and third movements differ from the first part both in tempo and style. These movements add interest and variety. The fourth movement is often more flamboyant, bringing the entire symphony to a stirring, harmonious conclusion.

Here is some Music Vocabulary.

Word	allegro con brio, adj.
Pronunciation	al-le-gro con bri-o
Definition	Lively with brilliance; a direction on how a musical composition should be performed

▶ *The orchestra began the allegro con brio third movement.*

Word	concerto, n.
Pronunciation	con-cer-to
Definition	A composition for a solo instrument (piano, violin, etc.) in three movements, accompanied by a symphonic orchestra

▶ *Mendelssohn's Violin Concerto in E Minor was Allison's favorite composition.*

Word	crescendo, n.
Pronunciation	cres-cen-do
Definition	A gradual increase in volume

▶ *The conductor of the symphony orchestra signaled the string section to begin a crescendo.*

Word	diminuendo, n.
Pronunciation	di-min-u-en-do
Definition	A gradual decrease in volume

▶ *The pianist lightened his touch as he began a diminuendo leading to the end of the piece.*

Word	fortissimo, adj.
Pronunciation	for-tis-si-mo
Definition	Very loud

▶ *The symphony ended with a grand fortissimo.*

Exercise 2: Write, Say, Define

Write the Musical Terms Vocabulary in your notebook. Study the pronunciation. Say the words. Write the definitions and indicate whether a word is a noun, a verb, or an adjective.

The Ballet

Bolshoi is a Russian word that means "grand." The Bolshoi Theater in Moscow was the birthplace of the famous classical Bolshoi Ballet. A classical ballet follows a rigid set of rules in terms of performance and costume. The ballerinas, or female dancers, wear toe shoes and tutus. Tutus are short or mid-length fluffy skirts made of layers and layers of sheer, gauzy fabric. The male dancers wear leotards and ballet slippers. A variety of other costumes are also worn. A ballet is set to music; like the opera, the ballet tells a story and consists of two or three acts. Instead of singing, ballet dancers enact the plot through movements that express varying emotions. Instead of a chorus, arias, and duets between the main characters as you hear in an opera, the ballet consists of scenes with many dancers on stage, solo numbers by the leading male and female performers, and a pas de deux. Performed by a male and a female dancer, the pas de deux, a French phrase meaning "steps for two," is very often a love scene. The dance movements can express tenderness, passion, and erotic sensuality. As in the opera, the music, by tempo and mood, influences what the dancers perform on the stage.

Future members of the Bolshoi undergo rigorous training from early childhood. Only promising students are accepted into the ballet school. The work is hard, demanding, physically painful, and exhausting. Dedicated pupils endure these hardships for the joy of dancing.

 Fact

Many musicians who composed symphonies and other compositions also wrote music for the ballet. The beloved *Nutcracker Suite, Sleeping Beauty,* and *Swan Lake* ballets are based on fairy tales and are all accompanied by beautiful orchestral music written by Peter Tchaikovsky.

Traditionally, a ballet vocabulary consists of French words and phrases that are used internationally. The Bolshoi Russian Ballet is no exception. In pre-revolutionary Russia, French was spoken by the nobility and elite society. In fact, it was the preferred language, its use dictated by etiquette. For this reason, the Ballet Vocabulary with one exception is derived from the French.

Word	arabesque, n.
Pronunciation	a-ra-besque
Definition	A ballet position in which the dancer stands on one leg and extends the body and one arm forward while the other leg and arm are raised and extended backward

▶ *Standing on one toe, the ballerina executed a perfect arabesque.*

Word	battement, n.
Pronunciation	bat-te-ment
Definition	A leap executed while beating the legs against each other

▶ *The audience applauded Michael's rapid battement.*

Word	choreographer, n.
Pronunciation	cho-re-og-rapher
Definition	The creator of moves and figures for a ballet

▶ *The success of a ballet depends on the imagination and skill of the choreographer.*

Word	corps de ballet, n.
Pronunciation	corps de bal-let
Definition	The members of a ballet company who do not perform solo numbers

▶ *The corps de ballet gave a sprightly performance.*

Word	grand jeté, n.
Pronunciation	grand je-té
Definition	A great leap

▶ *The grand jeté is usually executed by a male dancer in a series across the stage.*

Exercise 3: Write, Say, Define

Write the Ballet Vocabulary in your notebook. Study the pronunciation. Say the words. Write the definitions and indicate whether a word is a noun, a verb, or an adjective.

What You've Learned

The last three sections were an introduction to the fine art of music. Your vocabulary words were related to the opera, the symphony, and the ballet. In each instance, orchestral music plays an integral part regardless of whether it assumes a supporting role in an opera or a ballet performance or has the main role in a symphony.

A Visit to the Art Museum

The art that we see in an art museum consists of pictures, oils, watercolors, charcoal sketches, and pen-and-ink drawings. There may be sculptures and carvings, pottery and ancient artifacts discovered by archeologists. A walk through a museum can be a journey into history. The paintings and drawings and other pieces of art serve as milestones marking the history of human development and civilization.

Throughout the ages, artists have recorded life as they knew it. Beginning with the sketches of hunts and wild animals drawn by early humans upon the walls of their caves, we can trace century by century how people lived, what they wore, and what was culturally and socially significant at the time they produced their works of art. Cataclysmic events, natural disasters, and great storms, historic battles, shipwrecks, and the death scenes of famous individuals, along with saints, martyrs and the crucifixion of Christ, are dramatically depicted by the artwork in a museum.

Over the centuries, art has undergone tremendous changes. Like the clothes we wear, modern or contemporary art bears little resemblance to paintings that are four or five hundred years old. Your Art Vocabulary will name significant periods in the world of art, beginning with Byzantine paintings.

Here is a list of Art Vocabulary.

Word	Byzantine, adj.
Pronunciation	Byz-an-tine
Definition	Of or relating to the Byzantine Empire

▶ *Byzantine icons are religious paintings that consist of flat, rather dark images of Christ, the Madonna, and the saints against a gold background. Antique and contemporary icons can be seen in Greek and Russian Orthodox churches.*

Pronunciation	cubism, n.
Pronunciation	cub-ism
Definition	A school of modern art concerned with abstract and geometric representations rather than a realistic interpretation of nature

▶ *Cubism is an interesting art form, although it may be difficult to understand.*

Word	impressionism, n.
Pronunciation	im-pres-sion-ism
Definition	A new technique and approach to painting originating in France in the latter part of the nineteenth century

▶ *Renoir, Manet, and Monet were among the leaders of impressionism. Their paintings are still greatly admired and valued.*

Word	Renaissance, n.
Pronunciation	ren-ais-sance
Definition	The transition period between the Middle Ages and modern times characterized by a revival of artistic and intellectual achievement

▶ *During the Renaissance, in the fourteenth and fifteenth centuries, the art of painting flourished; to this day, we treasure the masterpieces of Leonardo da Vinci, Michelangelo, Raphael, and many other fine artists.*

Exercise 4: Write, Say, Define

Write the Art Vocabulary in your notebook. Study the pronunciation. Say the words. Write the definitions and indicate whether a word is a noun, a verb, or an adjective.

What You've Learned

It is hoped that this section roused an interest in seeing world-famous paintings and in tracing the history of art and humankind from early beginnings to modern times. If you already love art and enjoy visiting art museums, then you understand why everyone is encouraged to do so. Colors are the soul of paintings. Our next section will introduce you to colors.

Color Vocabulary

Nature is a vast, enduring, ever-changing panorama of color. If you look closely, you'll see delicate variations in color in a patch of grass, in shadow and light. A photograph can record with great beauty and accuracy a glorious sunset or a red rose adorned with a single dewdrop. Photography is indeed an art form that deserves recognition and appreciation. In this section, however, the focus is on how artists use color in their paintings.

 Essential

> In ancient times artists, potters, spinners and weavers, had to make their own paints and dyes. Nature provided many of these products. Berries, vegetables and other plants were used to make red, dark blue, and brown shades. Powdered lapis lazuli, a deep blue semiprecious stone, was widely used by Renaissance painters.

A masterpiece differs from a mediocre work in how an artist applies his or her paints to give texture or smoothness to a piece of fabric. It differs also in how the artist selects and mixes those paints to capture the subtle play between shadows and light. Furthermore, a true artist puts something of himself or herself into the work, something unique and recognizable that even the most skilled forger fails to duplicate.

Here is the Color Vocabulary.

Word	aureolin, n.
Pronunciation	au-re-o-lin
Definition	A bright, yellow pigment made from cobalt and potassium

▶ *Aureolin is used in watercolors and oil paints.*

Word	cobalt blue, adj.
Pronunciation	co-balt blue
Definition	A deep blue to greenish-blue pigment made of oxide of cobalt and aluminum

▶ *The artist's model wore a cobalt blue gown.*

Word	magenta, adj.
Pronunciation	ma-gen-ta
Definition	A strong purple-red pigment

▶ *The chemical discovery of magenta occurred about a hundred and fifty years ago.*

Word	nigrescence, n.
Pronunciation	ni-gres-cence
Definition	The process of becoming black or dark

▶ *The painting emphasized the nigrescence of the thundercloud.*

Word	vermilion, n.
Pronunciation	ver-mil-ion
Definition	A durable bright red pigment

▶ *Vermilion is obtained by grinding the mineral cinnabar into a fine powder.*

Exercise 5: Write, Say, Define

Write the Color Vocabulary in your notebook. Study the pronunciation. Say the words. Write the definitions and indicate whether a word is a noun, a verb, or an adjective.

The Essence of Poetry

The fine art of literature refers to all forms of literary writing: essays, stories, plays, fiction and nonfiction books. Poetry is a creative form of writing that is indeed a fine art. There are many types of poetry. The epic poem celebrates, in a grand style, mythological and actual historical events. A narrative poem tells a story in a somewhat simpler style. "The Midnight Ride of Paul Revere" by the American poet Henry Wadsworth Longfellow is a narrative poem.

An ode is a lyric poem. Most well-known poetry is lyrical. Lyric poems are sensitive in tone. They express the poet's personal feelings of love, yearning, sorrow, and happiness. An ode is a lyrical dedication to something or someone that the writer admires and loves. It describes how the subject of the ode affects the poet emotionally. Poetry can rhyme or not; poems that do not rhyme are referred to as blank verse. Rhyming or not, poetry's main distinguishing characteristic is its rhythm. Our heartbeat has a recognizable rhythm. A flying bird moves its wings rhythmically. The rower plying a skiff raises and dips her oars with a steady, rhythmic movement of arms and body. For a piece of literature to be a poem, it must have a definite repetitive rhythm. The rhythm is achieved by the identical stress of certain words or syllables and the length of the lines. Although the line length may vary, there must be a consistent pattern.

Fact

The word *lyric* as it is used in reference to a poetic style comes from the Greek and Latin noun for a stringed harp-like instrument called a lyre. Odes were first written to be sung to the accompaniment of a lyre. This was the origin of the term that now applies to romantic and poetically emotional poems.

Example 1: Iambic verse: The second syllable of the poem is stressed; from then on, every other syllable is also accented.

Beneath the spreading chestnut-tree
The village smithy stands;

The smith, a mighty man is he
With large and sinewy hands.

("The Village Blacksmith," by Henry Wadsworth Longfellow, 1839)

Note that lines one and three are longer (have more syllables) than lines two and four. This rhythmic pattern is continued throughout the poem.

Example 2: A poetic pattern in which the first syllable or word of the poem is stressed is called trochaic. The following two lines of a blank verse (unrhymed verse) illustrate a trochaic beat.

Bring me roses, blood-red roses
Bring me lilies, white as lace

("Requiem," Valentine Dmitriev)

The most significant difference between prose and poetry is that with one word or one line, the poet can tell a story, describe a scene, or reveal an emotion that would take a prose writer several paragraphs to achieve. This fact is the true essence, the soul, of poetry.

Example 3: In a short poem, William Wordsworth (1770–1850) describes a young orphan girl whom no one praised or loved. In the second stanza, Wordsworth describes the girl, calling her a "violet by a mossy stone," a single star when no other stars are visible. He concludes the poem with the following lines:

She lived unknown, and few could know
When Lucy ceased to be;
But she is in her grave, and, oh,
The difference to me!

In this last line, the whole story of the poet's sorrow is revealed. Secretly, it appears, he was in love with Lucy.

Here is some Poetic Vocabulary:

Word	alliteration, n.
Pronunciation	al-lit-er-a-tion
Definition	A series of two or more words with the same initial letter or sound; an effective literary or poetic device

▶ *The phrase "only a lone loon crying" uses the l sound as alliteration.*

Word	iambic, n.
Pronunciation	i-am-bic
Definition	A poem in which the second word or syllable in a line of poetry is stressed

▶ *"My country, 'tis of thee" is written with an iambic rhythm.*

Word	sonnet, n.
Pronunciation	son-net
Definition	A fourteen-line poem that has various rhyming schemes and follows a specific format

▶ *Shakespeare wrote many sonnets that are now well-known.*

Word	stanza, n.
Pronunciation	stan-za
Definition	A division of a poem that contains a certain number of lines of verse grouped in a definite scheme

▶ *This poem had sixteen lines and was divided into four stanzas with four verse lines in each stanza.*

Word	trochaic, n.
Pronunciation	tro-cha-ic
Definition	A rhythm that stresses the first syllable or word in a line of poetry

ᵘ *"Yankee Doodle went to town" illustrates the trochaic rhythm. The song begins with the accent on the first syllable of the word Yankee.*

Exercise 6: Write, Say, Define

Write the Poetic Vocabulary in your notebook. Study the pronunciation. Say the words. Write the definitions and indicate whether a word is a noun, a verb, or an adjective.

Final Review

With the conclusion of this section on fine arts, it is time to review the new words that have been added to your increasing knowledge of less familiar words.

Exercise 7: Complete the Words

Read the first letters of the following words. Complete the words by adding the missing letters.

1. a r __ __

2. b a s s o   p r o __ __ __ __ __

3. c o l o __ __ __ __ __ __

4. lib_____

5. over_____

6. allegro ___ b____

7. con_____

8. cres_____

9. dimi_____

10. fort_____

Exercise 8: Find the Missing Consonants
Read the following words and add the missing consonants.

1. ara__e___ue

2. ba___e_e___

3 c_o_eo__ap_e_

4. cor__ de _a__e_

5. g_a___ je_é

Exercise 9: Find the Missing Vowels
Read the following and add the missing vowels.

1. a_r__l_n

2. c _ b _ lt   bl _ _

3. m _ g _ nt _

4. n _ gr _ sc _ nc _

5. v _ rm _ l _ _ n

6. _ ll _ t _ r _ t _ _ n

7. _ _ m b _ c

8. s _ n n _ t

9. st _ n z _

10. tr _ ch _ _ c

Chapter 13
Potpourri: Emotions and Essentials

Most commonly, the word *potpourri* refers to a mixture of dried flower petals that give off a pleasant aroma. The term can also mean a literary production composed of miscellaneous parts. This chapter is so titled because the vocabulary will be a potpourri of words, relating to several different topics. You'll find words that are descriptive of feelings, emotions, and phobias as well as other essential terms.

Feelings and Emotions

Feelings and emotions are almost identical in context. However, there are subtle differences. A feeling is a bodily sensation. If you stub your toe, you feel pain. If it's a chilly day and you're not warmly dressed, you feel cold. These are physical sensations that can arouse an emotional response. If you had hurt your toe by banging it against a child's neglected toy, you might feel a sudden emotional surge of anger at your child's carelessness. Feeling cold, you might experience self-pity because you couldn't afford to buy a winter coat.

 Fact

> *Euphoria* originates from the Greek word *euphorien*, meaning good health. The word *euphoria* is also a term used in present day psychiatry in reference to an abnormal, exaggerated state of high spirits or cheerfulness. Such behavior may be a symptom of a bipolar disorder.

Emotions are involuntary physical responses to events in life. A blush, a laugh, an increased heart rate, sudden loss of color, and tears are examples of emotional reactions. An emotion may be fleeting or it may remain for days, or even years. A happy bride-to-be may be in an emotional state of excitement and joy for weeks before the wedding. A grieving widow may experience sadness and loss for months, if not years. The ability to feel enables a person to identify an emotion as something that is either positive or negative. It is when an individual represses an undesirable emotion (such as hidden anger, guilt, or self-hatred) that psychological damage can occur.

Positive Emotions Vocabulary

To begin, here are some words that are used to express positive, joyful emotions:

Word	ecstatic, adj.
Pronunciation	ec-stat-ic
Definition	Overjoyed; wildly happy

▶ *Susie was ecstatic when Andy proposed and gave her a ring.*

Word	elation, n.
Pronunciation	e-la-tion
Definition	Excitement; triumph; delight

▶ *When Ted was accepted by the college of his choice, he was filled with elation.*

Word	euphoria, n.
Pronunciation	eu-pho-ri-a
Definition	A feeling of health and physical well-being

▶ *Spring brought euphoria to the old farmer.*

Word	exhilaration, n.
Pronunciation	ex-hil-a-ra-tion
Definition	The state of being pleasantly excited and stimulated

▶ *As she skated across the frozen pond, she laughed with exhilaration.*

Word	exultant, adj.
Pronunciation	ex-ul-tant
Definition	Triumphant; marked by rejoicing

▶ *James was exultant when his novel became a bestseller.*

Exercise 1: Write, Say, Define

Write the Joyous Emotions Words in your notebook. Study the pronunciation. Say the words. Write the definitions and indicate whether a word is a noun, a verb, or an adjective.

Essential

> *Jealousy*, another word for *invidia*, is a strong and dangerous emotion. The poet John Dryden describes jealousy as "the jaundice of the soul." Jealousy is the emotion that drives Othello to murder his wife, Desdemona, in Shakespeare's drama *Othello*.

Negative Emotions Vocabulary

Things go wrong—a loved one dies, or we fail to attain a desired goal. Someone treats us badly and we become angry. Envy, hatred, fear, and embarrassment are human emotions that everyone experiences at one time or another. Problems arise, however, when a negative emotion becomes so deeply embedded in a person's consciousness that no other, more positive feelings are allowed to replace it. Chronic anger, grief, or feelings of low self-esteem can damage your health and ruin your life. The cure lies in acknowledging an injurious negative emotion, which permits you to discard it, and in extreme cases, seeking professional help.

Word	abhorrence, n.
Pronunciation	ab-hor-rence
Definition	A feeling of great dislike or loathing

▶ *The filthy task filled her with abhorrence.*

Word	desolate, adj.
Pronunciation	des-o-late
Definition	Lonely; abandoned

▶ *Marge was desolate when her lover left her.*

Word	invidia, n.
Pronunciation	in-vi-di-a
Definition	Envy; jealousy

▶ *Every time her sister had a date, Lily suffered pangs of invidia.*

Word	melancholia, n.
Pronunciation	mel-an-cho-li-a
Definition	A disorder characterized by despair and extreme chronic sadness

▶ *A psychiatrist treated Bill's melancholia.*

Word	umbrage, n.
Pronunciation	um-brage
Definition	Resentment; anger

▶ *Kate's umbrage over trifles put a strain on her marriage.*

Exercise 2: Write, Say, Define

Write the Negative Emotions Vocabulary in your note-book. Study the pronunciation. Say the words. Write the definitions and indicate whether a word is a noun, a verb, or an adjective.

Phobias

A phobia is an unreasonable, compulsive, persistent fear of any specific type of object, animal, insect, or situation. Having to face something that a person fears can produce a phobia anxiety attack. Such an attack may have a number of physical reactions: heart palpitations, breathlessness, weakness, an uncontrollable feeling of terror, and hysterical screaming. Anxiety and phobias are closely related. Stress and unresolved conflicts can lead to a chronic state of anxiety. We all experience stress, conflicts, and anxiety. In most cases these are temporary reactions to isolated events. Studying for a final exam can produce both stress and anxiety. Once the exam is passed, more positive emotions replace the stress and anxiety. Unfortunately, stressful, anxiety-producing situations may continue for months and years, seemingly without end. Children reared in dysfunctional, abusive homes exist in a state of chronic stress and anxiety. Soldiers in a drawn-out war suffer similar psychological pressures that often lead to a physical illness known as battle fatigue, shell shock, or mental and nervous breakdowns.

Individuals suffering from chronic anxiety may develop a phobia as a safety net. As long as they avoid the phobia-producing object, animal, or situation, they can repress their ever-present anxiety and lead a fairly stable life. However, when the person encounters the fear-inducing object, the repressed anxiety may erupt into a phobic panic attack. Ancient Greek and Latin scholars identified and named over two hundred different phobias. For the purpose of this section, the vocabulary will focus on ten of the most commonly encountered phobias.

 Fact

> Desensitization is a technique used by therapists in helping patients overcome their phobias. The goal is to substitute a fear reaction in the presence of the phobia-producing situation to one of calmness and relaxation. This retraining is achieved by small steps in a nonthreatening environment and is generally successful in eliminating the phobia. More information can be obtained via the Internet.

Word	Pronunciation	Fear of
acrophobia, n.	ac-ro-pho-bi-a	Heights
agoraphobia, n.	ag-o-ra-pho-bi-a	Open spaces
ailurophobia, n.	ai-lu-ro-pho-bi-a	Cats
arachnophobia, n.	a-rach-no-pho-bi-a	Spiders
autophobia, n.	au-to-pho-bi-a	Being alone
claustrophobia, n.	claus-tro-pho-bi-a	Confined spaces
cynophobia, n.	cy-no-pho-bi-a	Dogs
demophobia, n.	de-mo-pho-bi-a	Crowds
hemophobia, n.	he-mo-pho-bi-a	Blood
ophidiophobia, n.	o-phi-di-o-pho-bia	Snakes

Exercise 3: Write, Say, Define

Write the Phobia Vocabulary in your notebook. Study the pronunciation. Say the words. Write the definitions and indicate whether a word is a noun, a verb, or an adjective.

Essential Words

Until now, the words that you've been learning have been related to specific topics: health, business, legal, and medical. The purpose of this next section is to introduce ten additional essential words that should not be overlooked even though they do not belong in any one specific category.

Alert!

The word *mesmerize* is associated with Franz Mesmer (1734-1815), an Austrian physician, who was famous for inducing hypnotic states in people. Another source claims that Mesmer was falsely credited with having invented hypnotism. In any case, mesmerism remains symbolic of Franz Mesmer's experiments in the field of hypnosis.

Word	ambiance, n.
Pronunciation	am-bi-ance
Definition	The "feel" or atmosphere of a place

▶ *It was a small café, but its ambiance was charming.*

Word	deplorable, adj.
Pronunciation	de-plor-a-ble
Definition	Poorly done; unworthy; deserving of reproach

▶ *The mess in her kitchen was deplorable.*

Word	impertinent, adj.
Pronunciation	im-per-ti-nent
Definition	Rude; improper; irrelevant

▶ *Jack was fired for his impertinent remarks to a customer.*

Word	jocund, adj.
Pronunciation	joc-und
Definition	Cheerful; lighthearted

▶ *A man with a jocund personality is a welcome guest.*

Word	livid, adj.
Pronunciation	liv-id
Definition	Extremely angry; infuriated

▶ *Nancy was livid when she learned that her boyfriend was seeing another woman.*

Word	mesmerize, v.
Pronunciation	mes-mer-ize
Definition	To hypnotize; to hold one's attention

▶ *The magician mesmerized his audience.*

Word	misconstrue, v.
Pronunciation	mis-con-strue
Definition	To misunderstand; to misinterpret

▶ *Molly was warned not to misconstrue Ken's attention because he was known to be a philanderer.*

Word	obtuse, adj.
Pronunciation	ob-tuse
Definition	Having poor powers of intellect or observation

▶ *I must be obtuse; I can never remember where I parked the car.*

Word	parameter, n.
Pronunciation	pa-ram-e-ter
Definition	Limit or boundary

▶ *Within the parameters set by their mother, the children were free to play outside.*

Word	philanderer, adj.
Pronunciation	phi-lan-der-er
Definition	A man who flirts and exploits women but who can't or doesn't intend to marry

▶ *Helen had to admit that her brother was a philanderer.*

 Essential

> The word *livid*, which was defined in your vocabulary list as extremely angry, has other meanings. Originating from the Latin and French words *lividus* and *livide* that mean to be blue in color, *livid* came to signify bruised, discolored flesh such as black and blue as well as ashen or very pale. Because the color of an extremely angry person's face may turn white or red, it appears that *livid* came to denote anger in additions to its other definitions.

Exercise 4: Write, Say, Define

Write the Essential Words in your notebook. Study the pronunciation. Say the word. Write the definitions and indicate whether a word is a noun, a verb, or an adjective.

Clichés

Cliché (pronounced klee-shay) is the French word for "stereotype." In other words, it's something that is worn out through repetitive use. In English, *cliché* is used to describe phrases and expressions that have crept into a language to such an extent that they have lost their freshness and original meaning. Clichés are boring and trite, yet we continue to parrot them, scarcely aware of how they clutter our speech. The reason that clichés invade a language, spreading like a virus, is that someone once said something so clever or funny that it became popular. People began repeating the phrase, applying it to other situations. With continued use, the term became a cliché.

"Saved by the bell" is an example of a cliché. You've probably heard and used that expression yourself. I don't know how it originated. Perhaps a sports reporter invented the phrase in reference to a boxing bout. Now the phrase is used to describe any number of occasions when something happens to one's advantage.

Exercise 5: Complete the Cliché

Read the following lines and fill in the blanks, completing the phrases. The purpose of this exercise is to increase your awareness of these trite expressions. Anyone wishing to improve both verbal and written language skills must learn to avoid clichés.

Phrase	**Word**
It rained cats and	_____
Easy as	_____
Slept like a	_____
Flat as a	_____

Phrase	**Word**
Mad as a wet	_____
Stubborn as a	_____
Happy as a	_____
Better than a stick in your	_____
So hungry he could eat a	_____
Slower than molasses in	_____

To check your answers, although it may hardly be necessary, refer to the appendix.

Clichés are fun, and that is why they are so widely used, even though we no longer remember or know how or why they came to be. Make up your own clichés and keep them in your family, but refrain from using them in place of more refined speech and fresh, original literary endeavors.

Vulgarisms, Profanity, and Slang

Vulgarism refers to the type of speech that a poorly educated or careless person might use. The language is not necessarily coarse or offensive. Vulgar speech contains grammatical errors. Sometimes people misspeak even though in general they use good English. A woman, describing a fashionably dressed acquaintance says, "Oh, you should have seen Ida at that party. She was eloquently dressed." One may speak eloquently, but one dresses elegantly. Individuals who consistently misuse words are guilty of vulgarism.

Profanity is another matter. Cursing, swearing, and using four-letter words in reference to sexual behaviors, bodily functions, and anatomy fall in this category. Until they become part of everyday speech, profane or obscene words are basically power words that can shock, intimidate, or insult. That is their intent; for this reason, they should be used sparingly. Save them for an emergency as you would your last bullet against an encroaching enemy. It is deplorable and disheartening how obscenity has infiltrated our lives and language. Characters in books, actors in movies, rappers, men, women, and children shamelessly rattle off strings of ugly obscenities without thought or pause. There was a time when mothers washed their kids' mouths with soap for saying a disreputable word. Now mothers use words that would make a marine blush. Nevertheless, there is still a segment of society that will not tolerate profanity. Persons wishing to advance professionally in a chosen career should guard against slips of the tongue if profanity is part of their everyday vocabulary. Women, if they have picked up foul words from their male companions, should set higher standards for themselves and their family. In 1939 when the magnificent movie *Gone with the Wind* was released, audiences were shocked, almost traumatized, when Rhett Butler, played by Clark Gable, ended the movie with the following sentence: "Frankly, my dear, I don't give a *damn*!" People gasped. Never in their lives had they heard such a swear word in public. Too bad, we are so jaded now that we can listen to and say almost anything with impunity. The young of our time, when they begin using the *f* word and its numerous variations, may believe that they are daring and innovative. Little do they know. The word in question is ancient. It originated in France more than eight hundred years ago at the beginning of the thirteenth century.

Slang is not necessarily a lexicon of obscene words. Depending on which strata of society is speaking, some of the vocabulary may be offensive. Slang originated as the secret speech of tramps and thieves and other unsavory characters. Urban street gangs probably belong in that category.

Basically, slang that is not offensive is Teen Speak, and its main characteristic is that the words are short-lived. An alert mind invents or assigns a new meaning to a common word. Everyone latches onto the new expression and it's all the rage for several weeks. Then just as suddenly the fad fades, and a new slang word takes its place. At one time, *bad* meant good. As I write, *cool* and *chill* are widely used slang words, but I sense that their popularity is already coming to an end. Soon there will be other words to take their place in the teenager's made-up vocabulary.

> The first dictionary of slang was written over two hundred years ago. In 1785 a distinguished British antiquarian, Francis Grose, published *A Classic Dictionary of Vulgar Tongue*. In 1811 Grose published an expanded edition of this book titled *Lexicon Balatronicum: A Dictionary of Buckish Slang, Universal Wit, and Pickpocket Eloquence*. This book contains almost five thousand defined entries. The word *buckish* is defined as dapper, foppish.

Adolescence is a time of transition from childhood and dependence to independence and adulthood. Slang is the teenager's private speech. It sets teenagers apart from adults and authority. It's a step toward their own identity, and that's cool.

Exercise 6: Connect the Vulgarisms

Read the following phrases and substitute the following proper words for the vulgarisms. The proper words are *appendix, knew, collision, confession, fasted.*

Phrase	Word
I went to confusion.	_____
They took out my apprehendix.	_____

Phrase	Word
He fastened during Lent.	_____
I knewed the man.	_____
There was a collusion on Main.	_____

Final Review

Now it's time for exercises and word play as a final review of your new vocabulary words.

Exercise 7: Complete the Joyous and Negative Emotions words

Read the following and add the missing letters to complete the words.

1. e x u _ _ _ _ t

2. e x h i _ _ _ _ _ _ _ n

3. e c s t _ _ _ _

4. e l a _ _ _ _

5. e u p _ _ _ _ _

6. d e s _ _ _ _ _

7. a b h _ _ _ _ _ _ _

8. u m b _ _ _ _

9. i n v _ _ _ _

10. m e l a _ _ _ _ _ _ _

To check your answers, refer to the appendix.

Exercise 8: Phobias

Read the terms and draw a line matching the words with the correct definition.

Phobia	Fear of
acrophobia	Heights
agoraphobia	Spiders
ailurophobia	Open space
arachnophobia	Confined space
autophobia	Being alone
claustrophobia	Cats
cynophobia	Blood
demophobia	Snakes
hemophobia	Crowds
ophidiophobia	Dogs

To check your answers, refer to the appendix.

Exercise 9: Fill In the Missing Vowels

Read the following; fill in the missing vowel to complete the words.

1. ph __ l __ n d __ r __ r

2. p __ r __ m __ t __ r

3. __ b t __ s __

4. m __ s c __ n s t r __ __

5. l __ v __ d

6. m __ s m __ r __ z __

7. j __ c __ n d

To check your answers, refer to the appendix.

Exercise 10: Hidden Words
Read the following words and find at least ten hidden words in each of the terms. Write the hidden words in your notebook.

1. ambiance
2. deplorable
3. impertinent

How many hidden words did you find? Were you able to find more than ten in each parent word?

The next and final chapter of this book will introduce you to Latin and other foreign-language phrases that every educated person should know and understand.

Chapter 14
International Languages

In this final chapter, starting with Latin, you'll be introduced to a basic foreign-language vocabulary. An educated person is expected to be able to read, pronounce, and understand at least a few of these words and phrases. If you have traveled on business or as a tourist, some of the words may be familiar to you. Knowledge of other languages will not only help you communicate with and understand people of other cultures, but it will also teach you about the origins of your own language and culture.

Latin and the Roman Empire

As you studied the vocabulary lists in the preceding chapters, you may have noted how many of the words we know as English originated from Latin. This is not surprising. At the height of its glory, the Roman Empire was an octopus reaching out its tentacles north and south, east and west, invading and occupying far-flung territories. Wherever they went, the Romans left imprints of their language and culture. In A.D. 43 Romans invaded England, beginning an occupation that lasted until 410.

At the time of the Roman conquest, England was inhabited by Celts, a tall, blond race that originated in Europe. Archeological digs have uncovered artifacts of their culture in Halostalt, Austria. Historically, the Celts belonged to the Iron Age. Their weapons were made of iron, surpassing the weaker armaments of the Bronze Age. Traveling south, the Celts settled in France where they were known as the Gauls. Crossing the English Channel, Celts migrated to England and began calling themselves Britons.

During their occupation, the Romans built roads and towns and Hadrian's Wall, which was seventy-three miles long and divided England and Scotland. The purpose of the wall was to keep Scottish hordes from disrupting the Roman occupation. Inevitably, the Britons' language was influenced by the Latin spoken by the Roman troops. Nevertheless, the original Britons' language survived in spite of the infiltration of Roman speech. Still, as we know, Latin remains a powerful force. The law and the sciences still retain their specialized Latin lexicons.

Here are some Latin phrases.

Phrase	ad hoc, n.
Pronunciation	ad hoc
Definition	Formed for one specific purpose

▶ *An ad hoc committee was appointed to prepare a budget for the new school year.*

Phrase	carpe diem, n.
Pronunciation	car-pe di-em
Definition	A warning to seize the pleasures of the moment; literally, "seize the day"

▶ *Carpe diem means that we should live for the moment and not the future.*

Phrase	habeas corpus, n.
Pronunciation	ha-be-as cor-pus
Definition	Literally, "you have the body"

▶ *In law,* habeas corpus *is a writ, a court order, commanding the release of a person who is unlawfully imprisoned.*

Phrase	in forma pauperis, adj.
Pronunciation	in for-ma pau-per-is
Definition	Literally, "in the manner of a pauper"; poor

▶ *Being unable to pay court costs, the beggar was declared to be in forma pauperis.*

Phrase	sine qua non, n.
Pronunciation	si-ne qua non
Definition	An essential condition; literally, "without which not"

▶ *A happy ending is the sin qua non of a proper romance novel.*

Exercise 1: Write, Say, Define

Write the Latin Words list in your notebook. Study the pronunciations. Say the words. Write the definitions and indicate whether a word is a noun, a verb, or an adjective.

French Words and Phrases

France, known as Gallia and inhabited by the Gauls, was conquered by the Romans in 217. From that time, the Gauls, like the Britons, remained under Roman subjugation until the demise of the Roman Empire in the fifth century. Once again Latin infiltrated the language of the land, and we find French words originating from the Latin words of the victorious Romans.

Fact

> As was mentioned in a previous chapter, French was the elite language among the upper social classes in Russia. This was equally true in England. Well brought-up children were taught to speak French at an early age. If you were to read a historical Victorian novel set in England as well as in America you might be surprised at how many French words and phrases are embedded in the dialogues as well as the narrative.

Today we know France for its fine cuisine, excellent wine, haute couture, sophistication, and elegant language. France is also the homeland of famous impressionistic and contemporary painters, art galleries, operas, and architecture.

The secret of speaking good French lies in proper pronunciation. This may not be easy because the pronunciations can be tricky if you have not heard it spoken by an educated native of France. The first thing to remember is that the language is soft and flowing with few harsh sounds. The final n in a word, for example, is given a light nasal tone with no accent on the letter. It is also important to know that the final consonant in a word is not always pronounced. The word for cat is *chat*. To say it correctly you say, *shaw*, dropping the *t* at the end. If, however, the letter *e* follows the final consonant, then the consonant is pronounced. The word for father is *père*, and because there's an e at the end, you would say *pear*, stressing both the first and last letters. To make things more confusing, some words that end in consonants do not follow these rules. Turn your attention to the following phrases and practice your French.

Phrase	bon soir
Pronunciation	bone-sware
Definition	Good evening

▶ *"Bon soir," Colette said to her friends.*

Phrase	c'est la vie
Pronunciation	se-la-vee
Definition	That is life

▶ *"C'est la vie," Peirre said, looking at his flat tire.*

Phrase	faux pas

| Pronunciation | fo-pa |
| Definition | A social error |

Note: the final s in pas is not pronounced.

▶ *Henry committed a faux pas when he used the wrong fork at a formal dinner.*

Phrase	merci
Pronunciation	mer-see
Definition	Thank you

▶ *Even if you don't speak French, it's polite to say "merci" when you are in France.*

Phrase	vis-à-vis
Pronunciation	vee-za-vee
Definition	Face to face with

▶ *"Let's discuss this vis-à-vis."*

Phrase	voilà
Pronunciation	voi-là
Definition	Used to call attention or express satisfaction; behold; see there

▶ *"Voilà!" Judy exclaimed, showing off her diamond ring.*

Exercise 2: Write, Say, Define

Write the French vocabulary list in your notebook. Study the pronunciations. Say the words. Write the definitions in your notebook.

Learning German

Germany is the land of beer, polkas, stupendous Teutonic castles, and the music of great composers. The three *B*s—Bach, Beethoven, and Brahms—are well known. Bach's compositions for the organ and the harpsichord, Beethoven's and Brahms's piano and orchestral works will live forever. Equally immortal is the music of Haydn, Handel, Mozart, Wagner, and many other German and Austrian composers.

Millions of people speak German. The language is spoken in Germany, Austria, Switzerland, South America, South Africa, and Australia. German is an interesting language with a long history of development. Like most European language, it has Latin roots, but basically German is a blend of words originating from the vocabularies of Germanic tribes that lived in eastern and northern parts of Germany. Later in history, Scandinavia and even Icelandic lexicons were added to the mix. It was in the late nineteenth century that the language became the modern German that is spoken today.

Phrase	auf Wiedersehen
Pronunciation	auf Wie-der-se-hen
Definition	An expression used to express farewell

▶ *Herr Dretsch kissed Polly's hand and said, "Auf Wiedersehen."*

Phrase	danke schön
Pronunciation	dan-ke shun
Definition	Used to express thanks

▶ *Traveling in Germany, Pat learned to say* danke schön.

Phrase	gesundheit
Pronunciation	ge-sund-heit
Definition	Used to wish good health after someone sneezes; literally, "health"

▶ *Whenever John sneezed, his German grandmother always said* Gesundheit.

Phrase	guten morgen
Pronunciation	gu-ten mor-gen
Definition	Used to wish good morning

▶ *"Guten morgen," the German teacher said to her students.*

Exercise 3: Write, Say, Define
Write the Germans words in your notebook. Study the pronunciations. Say the words. Write the definitions.

Viva Italia
By now, you should realize that the formation of a language is an ongoing process. The English that was spoken and written in the thirteenth and fourteenth centuries would be scarcely comprehensible to us now without specialized study of medieval literature. Without a doubt, the reverse would be equally true. The English we speak today with its vast technological lexicon would be meaningless to our ancestors. Similar changes, mutations, exist between the classical Latin pertaining to the period of the Roman Empire's glory and present-day Italian. Although

it is a fact that Italian descended from Latin, there were ongoing changes in the spoken Latin long before it evolved into the Italian of modern Italy. This metamorphosis began with the population's simplification of spoken Latin, especially in reference to the complex grammar of classical Latin.

Many factors affect the development of a language, and many factors contributed to the fall of the Roman Empire. In addition to sustained attacks by new civilizations that plundered Rome's treasures and decimated its army and population, there was decay within the empire itself. A decline in morals, public health issues, political corruption, and other national ills weakened Roman power.

 Fact

French, Spanish and Italian are languages that have strong Latin roots, especially the latter two. If you are able to speak either Spanish or Italian, the two languages are so similar that you should have no difficulty making yourself understood, even though you speak only one of the languages in question.

During the Renaissance, Italy was rebuilt as a nation of art and science; this was the transitional period that led Italy and Europe into the future. A visitor to Italy has much to see and learn. After a day of viewing the ancient marvels, and after basking on it's the beaches, nothing is more enjoyable than a delicious Italian meal.

Here, in North America, many words relating to Italian cuisine have become part of our daily speech. Your Italian Vocabulary will focus on expanding your knowledge of such terms.

Here is some Cuisine Vocabulary.

Phrase	antipasto caldo
Pronunciation	an-ti-pa-sto cal-do
Definition	Hot assorted appetizers

▶ *They began their meal with an antipasto* caldo.

Phrase	gamberi freddi
Pronunciation	gam-be-ri fred-di
Definition	Shrimp cocktail

▶ *Anita ordered* gamberi freddi.

Phrase	gnocchi
Pronunciation	gnoc-chi
Definition	Dumplings made of flour, potatoes, or semolina

▶ *Alex ordered a serving of gnocchi.*

Phrase	melanzane alla rottatini
Pronunciation	mel-an-za-ne al-la rot-ta-ti-ni
Definition	Eggplant stuffed with ricotta cheese

▶ *The* melanzane alla rottatini *was delicious*.

Phrase	vongole
Pronunciation	von-go-le
Definition	Clams

▶ *The menu offered fresh* vongole.

Exercise 4: Write, Say, Define

Write the Cuisine Vocabulary in your notebook. Study the pronunciations. Say the words. Write the definitions.

Spain and Its Languages

In the early fifteenth century, Spain, the motherland of the Spanish language, was a world power. Navigators like Columbus were crossing the oceans, seeking wealth and new territories, and conquering the inhabitants of ancient civilizations in Mexico and South America. Inevitably, the Spaniards brought their language and Christianity. Today there are more than thirty Spanish-speaking countries. In fact, Spanish is the third most widely spoken language in the world. Nevertheless, there are differences between the Spanish spoken in Mexico City and that spoken in Buenos Aires. An even greater difference in pronunciation and word usage exists between the Castilian Spanish in Madrid and the Spanish of Mexico and Latin America.

 Essential

Under Franco's Fascist dictatorship the native Catalan language was forbidden. Catalan was no longer taught in schools, and any other use of the language was not allowed. Once the dictatorship ended and democracy was restored, Catalan was again spoken freely, although the majority of people living in Barcelona are bi-lingual and speak both Catalan and Spanish.

Within Spain itself, there are regions where six other lesser-used languages are spoken. One of these autonomous regions is Catalonia. Barcelona, located on the eastern coast of Spain, is the capital of Catalonia, and Catalan, spoken by 6,000,000 people, is an official national language. Catalan is also spoken in several other areas of Spain, the Balearic Islands, Sardinia, and parts of both Italy and France.

Your Spanish Vocabulary will give you common Castilian words, easily understood by any Spanish-speaking person regardless of whether you are in Spain or in a Latin American country.

Phrase	buenos días
Pronunciation	bue-nos dí-as
Definition	Used to wish good morning

▶ Buenos días *is a polite greeting.*

Phrase	de nada
Pronunciation	de na-da
Definition	An expression that means "you're welcome"

▶ *"De nada," said Juanita when I thanked her for the gift.*

Phrase	Mi casa es su casa
Pronunciation	mi ca-sa es su ca-sa
Definition	A greeting meaning, "my house is your house"

▶ *"Mi casa es su casa," Maria said to her Mexican friend.*

Phrase	por favor
Pronunciation	por fa-vor

Definition	Please

▶ *Sam asked for a cup of coffee and added, "Por favor."*

Word	vaya con Dios
Pronunciation	va-ya con Di-os
Definition	Literally, "go with God"

▶ *"Vaya con Dios," the boy's mother blessed her son as he left for school.*

Exercise 5: Write, Say, Define
Write the Spanish Words list in your notebook. Study the pronunciation. Say the words. Write the definitions.

Russian Words
Russia is a vast territory, and its inhabitants are made up of numerous ethnic groups. There are people of Mongolian and Tartar descent. There are Muslims and people of Jewish faith, but the majority are Russian, a Slavic race. Serbs, Poles, Albanians, Czechs, and Ukrainians belong in this category. The Russian alphabet is Cyrillic, an old Slavic alphabet based mainly on Greek. Russian and Greek religions are also similar. The Russian Orthodox religion is the national faith of that nation. Prior to the Russian Revolution in 1917, the Russian people were very religious. There were many churches. These magnificent structures had gilded domes, topped with golden crosses.

Under Communist rule, religion was banned. Churches were destroyed or seized for purposes other than religious rites. Despite the bans, the majority of the people secretly clung to their faith. Now that Communists are no longer in power, churches are restored and the faithful are free to celebrate Christmas and Easter and other holy days.

 Essential

> Some Russians living in the United States, Canada, and other countries still celebrate Easter in the traditional way. They attend Russian Orthodox churches and spend hours baking *kulitches* in tall juice cans. Using their great-grandmother's recipes they make *paskhas* and other Easter delicacies.

Traditionally, after a long winter, Easter is a favorite time for worship and celebration. On Easter Sunday, every household is ready for guests. Tables are laden with appetizers, special dishes, and Easter desserts. *Paskha* is the Russian word for Easter. Your vocabulary will consist of words pertaining to that religious holiday.

Word	gosti, n.
Pronunciation	gho-stee
Definition	Guests

▶ *When the* gosti *arrived, Tanya was ready to welcome them.*

Word	ikra, n.
Pronunciation	ee-kra
Definition	Caviar

▶ Ikra *is served on dark bread.*

Word	kulitch, n.
Pronunciation	koo-lee-ch
Definition	A sweet, tall, cylindrical Easter bread

▶ *A* kulitch *is baked only once a year, for Easter.*

Word	paskha, n.
Pronunciation	pas-kha
Definition	Easter or a sweet Easter dessert made out of cottage cheese and shaped into a tall pyramid

▶ *The Easter* paskha *stood like a white pyramid in the center of the table.*

Word	zakuski, n.
Pronunciation	zah-koo-ski
Definition	Appetizers

▶ *Guests were offered pickled herring and caviar* zakuski.

Exercise 6: Write, Say, Define

Write the Russian Words list in your notebook. Study the pronunciation. Say the words. Write the definitions.

Final Review

It is suggested that you make your own review of the preceding foreign words and phrases. Reread this chapter or go through your notebook; study and say the words.

Share your new knowledge with your children and family members. Insert foreign words as you speak.

Your Improved Vocabulary

Congratulations! By now you've had the opportunity of expanding your vocabulary by 400 words, including 30 foreign words and phrases. Depending on your personal self-improvement goals, lifestyle, and occupation, some of the words in this book will become your friends and you will use them with increased frequency and confidence. Other words will remain nodding acquaintances. That's all right. You know where to locate them should the need arise; moreover, these words will not be strangers regardless of whether they are spoken or printed in a book or magazine. Do not allow the completion of this volume to be the end of your journey and your search for a wider vocabulary. Seek out new words and let the adventure of discovery and appreciation of the richness of a language be a delightful, unending journey.

Appendix
Exercise Answer Key

Chapter 1

Exercise 1

arduous	Stubborn	F
diligence	Constant effort	T
echelon	Loud echo	F
inept	Awkward	T
egalitarian	Fair person	T

Exercise 4

inundate	To flood	T
meticulous	Made of metal	F
negligence	Drowsiness	F
tedium	Boredom	T
temerity	Shyness	F

Exercise 6

apparel	Clothing	T
epicure	Beauty treatment	F
fetid	Greek cheese	F
haute couture	Fancy meal	F
memorabilia	Things worthy of remembrance	T

Exercise 8

amortize	Embalm	F
collateral	Property/money offered to ensure repayment	T
encumbrance	Embarrassment	F
fiduciary	Embezzlement	F
garnishment	Decoration	T

Exercise 10

colloquial	Somber	F
conviviality	A friendly gathering	T
frivolity	Lighthearted behavior	T
jocular	Vein in the neck	F
libation	A drink	T

Exercise 11

1. libation	4.	colloquial
2. jocular	5.	frivolity
3. conviviality		

Exercise 13

appellation	Title	T
approbation	Disapproval	F
decorum	Riot	F
disparagement	Verbal abuse	T
filial	Relating to children's relationships to their parents	T

Exercise 15 (Answers may vary.)

arduous	Simple
inept	Skilled
diligence	Laziness
egalitarian	Unfair
tedium	Excitement
meticulous	Careless
negligence	Attention
temerity	Shyness

Exercise 16 (Answers may vary.)

apparel	Clothing
fetid	Smelly
haute couture	High fashion
memorabilia	Valuables
amortize	Repay
collateral	Security
garnishment	Decoration
encumbrance	Hindrance

Chapter 2

Exercise 1

vacuous	Huge	F
vehement	Strong emotion	T
vestige	Garment	F
vicarious	Lively	F
voracious	Greedily hungry	T

Exercise 3

tantamount	Equal to	T
technocracy	Form of government	T
theocentric	Circular	F
thespian	Actor	T
tome	Small tent	F

Exercise 5

arctic	actic	r
recognize	reconize	g
government	goverment	n
February	Febuary	r
commensurate	commesurate	n

Exercise 6

iniquity	inquity	i
innocuous	innocous	u
obsequious	obsequous	i
penultimate	penutimate	l
rudimentary	rudmentary	i

Exercise 8

1. <u>ab</u>-di-cate
2. <u>ab</u>-er-<u>ra</u>-tion
3. car-<u>tel</u>
4. <u>des</u>-pot-ism
5. ser-en-<u>dip</u>-i-ty

Exercise 10

1. I need advice. Can you help me?
2. He gave me good advice.
3. I hope my attorney will advise me.
4. I will try to advise you.
5. The effect of the fire was terrifying.
6. She wondered how the fire would affect her parents.
7. Your kind words affect me deeply.
8. The effect of his speech was negligible.
9. The boy worked on his essay all afternoon.
10. The miner went to assay his gold nugget.
11. The man hurried to assay his ore findings.
12. Johnny wrote a fine essay.
13. The convoy left at dawn.
14. Please convey my regards to your father.
15. I tried to convey the urgency to my sister.
16. How can I convey this to him?

Exercise 11

1. <u>ob</u>-ject
2. ob-<u>ject</u>

Exercise 12

1. Market-controlling organization: cartel
2. Deviation from the standard: aberration
3. Resign a high position: abdicate
4. Happy coincidence: serendipity
5. Dictatorship: despotism

Exercise 13

1. tome
2. vestige
3. voracious
4. vicarious
5. thespian
6. vehement
7. tantamount
8. vacuous
9. theocentric
10. technocracy

Exercise 14

1. advice   advise
2. effect   affect
3. essay   assay
4. convey   convoy
5. complement   compliment

Exercise 15

1. iniquity
2. innocuous
3. obsequious
4. penultimate
5. rudimentary

Chapter 3

Exercise 2

1. ate	eat
2. went	go
3. spoke	speak
4. was	is
5. were	are
6. slept	sleep
7. had	have
8. read	read
9. verified	verify
10. fought	fight

Exercise 3

1. play	played
2. lay	laid
3. run	ran
4. grow	grew
5. leave	left
6. try	tried
7. fly	flew
8. know	knew
9. glow	glowed
10. expect	expected

Exercise 5

1. She and he are good friends.
2. I shall vote for the person I want.
3. The man who phoned me is my uncle.

4. Blessed are they who pray.
5. Who shall I say is calling?
6. The horse hurt its leg.
7. He and they caught a fish.
8. Whom will you marry?
9. He and she are coming soon.
10. Give this to whoever comes first.

Exercise 7

1. I sat by them.
2. Come, sit beside me.
3. This is for you and him.
4. The present was from her.
5. He will go with them/him/her. (Any of these pronouns would be correct.)

Exercise 10

1. The definition of a word in a dictionary: denotation
2. The implied meaning of a word: connotation
3. The study of word origins: etymology
4. No longer in use: obsolete
5. Recalling the past: retrospection
6. Refers to the present: contemporary
7. The theory of keeping up with the times: modernism
8. The meaning of things, especially words: semantics
9. Ancient times: antiquity
10. Grammatical relationship and arrangement of words: syntax

Exercise 11

1.	advent	5.	posterior	9.	hoi polloi
2.	eventuality	6.	subjugate	10.	subservient
3.	forebode	7.	maladroit		
4.	imminent	8.	servitude		

Exercise 13

1.	linguist	3.	lexicon	5.	vernacular
2.	philology	4.	morphology		

Chapter 4

Exercise 1

1. He has a new car.
2. He goes to work every day.
3. She got many phone calls.
4. We are going away.
5. A good student does his homework every night.

Exercise 2

1. He got/has the flu.
2. The storms were scary.
3. That girl does hard work.
4. I am tired tonight.
5. They go to the movies every week.

Exercise 4

1. I'm   I am
2. you've   you have

3. he's   he is
4. isn't   is not
5. doesn't   does not
6. don't   do not
7. can't   cannot
8. won't   will not
9. you're   you are
10. that'll   that will

Exercise 6

1. I can't do it no how.   I can't do it at all.
2. He don't know no better.   He doesn't know any better.
3. I don't got no money.   I don't have any money.
4. She won't never do it.   She will never do it.
5. They don't know nothing.   They don't know anything.

Exercise 8

1. Lie down, Fido.
2. He lay in bed all day.
3. I was lying on the sofa when the phone rang.

Exercise 10

1. nonentity   4. noncommittal
2. noncompliance   5. nonchalant
3. nonfeasance

Exercise 11

assiduous	Lazy	F
erudite	Educated	T
omniscience	The faculty of knowing everything	T

cognition	Machinery	F
fabrication	Dressmaking	F
prevaricate	To lie	T
recumbent	Obese	F
benighted	Unenlightened	T
consolidate	Unite	T
integration	Separation	F

Exercise 12

1. erudite	5. unschooled	9. recline
2. intelligentsia	6. incorporate	10. supine
3. impercipient	7. copulation	
4. nescience	8. ballad	

Chapter 5

Exercise 1

1.	epiglottis	throat
2.	esophagus	chest
3.	Eustachian tube	ear
4.	clavicle	collarbone
5.	pectoral muscle	chest
6.	pituitary gland	brain
7.	renal artery	kidney
8.	sternum	chest

Exercise 3

Diarrhea, vomiting	Gastroenteritis
Dizziness	Vertigo
Muscle weakness, joint stiffness, pain	Polymyalgia rheumatica
Skin rash	Dermatitis
Wheezing	Asthma

Exercise 5

cardiologist, n.	car-di-ol-o-gist	heart
dermatologist, n.	der-ma-tol-o-gist	skin
gynecologist, n.	gy-ne-col-o-gist	women's health
internist, n.	in-ter-nist	internal organs and systems
neurologist, n.	neu-rol-o-gist	nervous system
oncologist, n.	on-col-o-gist	cancer
ophthalmologist, n.	oph-thal-mol-o-gist	eyes
orthopedic surgeon, n.	or-tho-pe-dic surgeon	bones
otorhinolaryngologist, n.	o-to-rhi-no-lar-yn-gol-o-gist	ear, nose, and throat
pediatrician, n.	pe-di-a-tri-cian	children
podiatrist, n.	po-di-a-trist	feet

Exercise 7

aphasia	Loss of appetite	F
audiologist	Evaluates hearing loss	T
pathologist	Gives massages	F
physiotherapist	Gives IQ tests	F

Exercise 9

angiography	blood vessels
bronchoscopy	lungs
cardiac catheterization	heart
echography	internal organs
endoscopy	stomach

Exercise 11

caries	Periodontist	F
gingivitis	Family dentist	F
malocclusion	Orthodontist	T

Exercise 13

1. caries
2. gingivitis
3. periodontist
4. orthodontist
5. aphasia
6. pathologist
7. epiglottis
8. clavicle
9. esophagus

Exercise 14

1. Eustacian tubes
2. pituitary gland
3. renal artery
4. sternum
5. pectoral
6. vertigo
7. asthma
8. gastroenteritis
9. dermatitis
10. endoscopy

Exercise 15

1. Teeth: malocclusion
2. Lungs: bronchoscopy
3. Blood vessels: angiography
4. Heart: cardiac catheterization
5. Women's health: gynecologist

Chapter 6

Exercise 1

1. amniotic fluid
2. amniocentesis   diagnostic procedure

3. eclampsia — danger signal
4. ectopic pregnancy — fertilized egg doesn't enter the uterus
5. pyelitis — kidney inflammation

Exercise 3

1. breech presentation — Baby appears buttocks first
2. cesarean section — Surgery
3. episiotomy — Vaginal incision
4. occipital presentation — Baby appears face-up
5. neonate — Newborn

Exercise 5

1. altruistic — selfish
2. innovative — unimaginative
3. perceptive — unaware
4. precocious — delayed
5. vivacious — lethargic

Exercise 7

1. capricious — stable
2. contentious — agreeable
3. lachrymose — happy
4. lethargic — energetic
5. obstreperous — quiet

Exercise 10

1. autocratic — egalitarian
2. egocentric — open-minded

3. inflexible   tolerant
4. laissez-faire   involved
5. morose   cheerful

Exercise 12

1. affinity   alienation
2. cynosure   negligence
3. empathy   indifference
4. forbearance   impatience

Exercise 14

1. ectopic
2. neonate
3. amniotic fluid
4. episiotomy
5. amniocentesis
6. occipital presentation
7. pyelitis
8. eclampsia
9. breech presentation

Exercise 15

1. altruistic
2. innovative
3. perceptive
4. precocious
5. vivacious
6. contentious
7. obstreperous
8. lethargic
9. lachrymose
10. capricious

Exercise 16

1. dictatorial   autocratic
2. self-centered   egocentric
3. permissive   laissez-faire
4. gloomy   morose
5. natural attraction affinity
6. insight, compassion empathy

7.	tolerance	forbearance
8.	setting an example, guidance	cynosure

Chapter 7

Exercise 1

ascension	The rising of a celestial body	T
asteroid	A star	F
celestial	Angelic, heavenly	T
cerulean	Sky-blue	T
constellation	A group of stars	T
equinox	The first day of winter	F
meridian	A body of water	F
moon	Revolves around the sun	F
planetarium	The study of astrology	F
satellite	An orbiting celestial body	T

Exercise 5

1. Antibiotics can cure a cold.	F
2. Leprosy is caused by bacteria.	T
3. A vaccine can prevent rabies in animals.	T
4. A virus, herpes simplex, causes cold sores.	T
5. Ticks and mosquitoes can carry infectious diseases.	T

Exercise 8

1.	ascension	6.	equinox
2.	asteroid	7.	meridian
3.	celestial	8.	moon
4.	cerulean	9.	planetarium
5.	constellation	10.	satellite

Exercise 9

1. artifact
2. eolith
3. fossil
4. Homo sapiens
5. Stone Age
6. Paleolithic Age
7. Neolithic Age

Exercise 10

1. benthology
2. echinoderm
3. medusa
4. plankton
5. thermocline
6. immunize
7. microbiology
8. staphylococcus
9. streptococcus

Exercise 11

1. A wispy cloud	cirrus
2. A large cloud seen in fair weather	cumulus
3. A storm cloud	thundercloud
4. Steam or a hazy substance	vapor

Chapter 8

Exercise 3

A codicil is a handwritten note.	F
An executor is named in a will.	T
A holographic will is a copy.	F
When a person dies intestate, he dies where he was born.	F

Exercise 4

arbitrate	To argue	F
bona fide	A French term	F

common carrier	A business that transports passengers	T
damages	Payment for harm or loss	T
trespass	Complain	F

Exercise 7

arraignment	Judge's robe	F
commutation	Jurors' discussion	F
deposition	Sworn testimony	T

Exercise 9

1. abandonment
2. adultery
3. alimony
4. bigamy
5. custody
6. separation
7. abscond
8. embezzle
9. foreclose
10. forgery

Exercise 10

1. prenuptial   agreement
2. common   carrier
3. assault and   battery
4. aggravated   assault
5. holographic   will

Exercise 11

1. codicil
2. executor
3. intestate
4. arbitrate
5. bona fide
6. expunge
7. trespass
8. felony

Chapter 9

Exercise 7

1. ascertain
2. augment
3. buttress
4. coalesce
5. commensurate
6. competence
7. complaisant
8. expertise
9. indicative
10. interactive

Exercise 8

1. beleaguered
2. collusion
3. gamut
4. onus
5. opprobrium
6. gumption
7. glean
8. inculcate
9. laud
10. tutelage

Exercise 9

angry	belligerent
fair exchange	reciprocity
self-confident	assertive
finalize	consummate
yielding	concession

Exercise 10

nepotism	Hatred	F
commiserate	Ignore	F
innate	Inborn trait	T
cohort	A joke	F
nebulous	Vague	T

Chapter 10

Exercise 4

bacchanal	Card game	F
centennial	A hundredth anniversary	T
commemoration	Celebration in remembrance	T
jubilee	A dessert	F
matriculation	Admission to college	T
nuptials	Small rodents	F

Exercise 8

1. benevolence
2. charitable
3. solicitous
4. philanthropy
5. magnanimity

6. iniquitous
7. malicious
8. ruthless
9. transgression
10. vindictive

Exercise 10

1. grievous
2. disconsolate
3. nuptials
4. matriculation

5. bacchanal
6. centennial
7. commemoration

Exercise 11

1. calamity
2. catastrophe
3. conflagration

4. deluge
5. tempest
6. jubilee

Chapter 11

Exercise 3

acrimonious	friendly
mendacious	truthful
pugnacious	sweet
salacious	pure
sycophant	sincere

Exercise 8

1. disheveled	4. tawdry	7. harridan
2. unkempt	5. sloppiness	8. repugnant
3. slovenly	6. corpulent	9. ungainly

Exercise 9

1. acrimonious	4. salacious
2. mendacious	5. pugnacious
3. sycophant	6. believability

Exercise 10

1. elegant	4. impeccable
2. fastidious	5. Adonis
3. immaculate	6. enchanting

Exercise 11

Graceful; pliant	lithesome
Physical beauty	pulchritude
A quality of leadership; appeal	charisma
Suave; charming; attractive	winsome

Chapter 12

Exercise 7

1. aria
2. basso profundo
3. coloratura
4. libretto
5. overture
6. allegro con brio
7. concerto
8. crescendo
9. diminuendo
10. fortissimo

Exercise 8

1. arabesque
2. battement
3. choreographer
4. corps de ballet
5. grand jeté

Exercise 9

1. aureolin
2. cobalt blue
3. magenta
4. nigrescence
5. vermilion
6. alliteration
7. iambic
8. sonnet
9. stanza
10. trochaic

Chapter 13

Exercise 5

It rained cats and dogs.
Easy as pie.
Slept like a log.
Flat as a pancake.
Mad as a wet hen.
Stubborn as a mule.
Happy as a clam.
Better than a stick in your eye.

So hungry he could eat a horse.
Slower than molasses in January.

Exercise 6

I went to confession.
They took out my appendix.
He fasted during Lent.
I knew the man.
There was a collision on Main.

Exercise 7

1. exultant
2. exhilaration
3. ecstatic
4. elation
5. euphoria
6. desolate
7. abhorrence
8. umbrage
9. invidia
10. melancholia

Exercise 8

acrophobia	Heights
agoraphobia	Open space
ailurophobia	Cats
arachnophobia	Spiders
autophobia	Being alone
claustrophobia	Confined space
cynophobia	Dogs
demophobia	Crowds
hemophobia	Blood
ophidiophobia	Snakes

Exercise 9

1. philanderer
2. parameter
3. obtuse
4. misconstrue
5. livid
6. mesmerize
7. jocund